The
Goddess in India

The Goddess in India

THE FIVE
FACES
OF THE
ETERNAL
FEMININE

Devdutt Pattanaik

INNER TRADITIONS
ROCHESTER, VERMONT

Inner Traditions International
One Park Street
Rochester, Vermont 05767
www.InnerTraditions.com

Copyright © 2000 Devdutt Pattanaik

LIBRARY OF CONGRESS CATALOGING-IN-PUBLICATION DATA

Pattanaik, Devdutt.
The goddess in India : the five faces of the eternal feminine / Devdutt Pattanaik.
p.   cm.
Includes bibliographical references.
ISBN 0-89281-807-7
1. Goddesses, Hindu. 2. Goddesses—India. 3. Women—Religious aspects—Hinduism.
4. Hinduism—Doctrines. I. Title.

BL1216.P37 2000
294.5'2114—dc21
00-024425

Printed and bound in Korea

10   9   8   7   6   5   4   3   2   1

Text design by Kristin Camp. Text layout by Virginia Scott-Bowman.
This book was typeset in Goudy with Bellevue as the display typeface.

Grateful acknowledgment to the following:
Archeological Survey of India, for Lajja-gauri, p. 5; Vishnu and Laxmi, p. 9; Women in amorous embrace, p. 12; Vishnu in the form of a boar, p. 16; Mother with child, p. 41; Princess in her toilet, p. 46; Tree nymph, p. 52; Vishnu with nymph and monk, p. 60; Courtesan and sage, p. 68; Laxmi and Vishnu, p. 104; Palmprints, p. 117; Nymph adorning herself, p. 124; Yogini holding skull-mace, p. 125; Matrikas, p. 132; Durga, p. 142; Three forms of the mother-goddess, p. 151

Kelkar Museum, Pune, for Laxmana and Surpanaka, p. 88; Sita and Laxmana, p. 90; Sita's chastity being tested, p. 113; Worship of the tulsi plant, p. 116

Private collections, for Ardhanari, p. 17; Man with three women, p. 35; Man and woman in amorous embrace, 45; Women dancing with Krishna, p. 84; Metal effigy of Renuka-Yellamma, p. 137; Kali, p. 149; Chinnamastika, p. 154

For Sabitri, Seema, and Shami,
the three women in my life

Contents

Why This Book?

India has given the world the Hindu worldview, a way of looking at life that is quite different from the Judeo-Christian-Islamic scheme of things. Hindu scriptures make no mention of original sin. There is no talk of fall or redemption. No Eve is held responsible for the loss of paradise. No god decrees that man shall rule over woman. Instead, powerful and awe-inspiring goddesses are enshrined in Hindu temples. Why, then, is Hindu society patriarchal? Why are women described by Hindu lawmakers as temptations to be veiled and shrews to be tamed?

This book seeks the answer in stories held sacred by the Hindus. Like all sacred lores, sacred Hindu lore is a much-revered gift handed down by ancestors that gives an identity to a people, a worldview to a culture, and a frame of reference to a civilization. It forms the foundation of rituals, customs, and traditions. It gives the *why* of things. Just as tales of Lilith, Eve, Jael, Judith, Jezebel, Ruth, Salome, and Mary express the Abrahamic attitude toward women, so do tales of women from sacred Hindu lore capture Hindu views on womanhood.

Beyond the din of masculine sagas, the sacred literature of the Hindus is filled with plots palpating with feminine dreams and themes grating with female fury. There are tales of goddesses who strike children with fever, nymphs who seduce sages, celestial virgins who run free in forests, and chaste wives who fling themselves on funeral pyres to become guardians of feminine virtue. There are ballads smeared with menstrual blood and songs fragrant with forbidden love. Somewhere in these narratives beats the heart of the ageless Hindu woman—dreams of the inner courtyard, unshed burdens of her womb.

This book retells tales of the chastity, fertility, seduction, and sacrifice that have made Hindu women divine. It also brings together legends of princesses, queens, amazons, heroines, and harlots—women not so divine—who lived, loved, and delivered life into Jambudvipa, the sacred rose-apple continent of India. From the recurring motifs and plots emerge five faces of the eternal feminine that give a better understanding of the traditional Hindu woman—seated to the left of her husband, dressed in red, worshipped as goddess, feared as temptress.

Each tale in the book has germinated in Indian soil. All have festered in the heat, shivered in the rain. Over the centuries they have been baked with bricks in the cities of the Indus; hidden in caves by dark-skinned forest tribes; scented by floral offerings of the Dravidians; crushed under the chariots of the Aryans; singed in the sacred altars of Brahmins; challenged by the wisdom of the Buddha and the Tirthankara; cut by the blades of Greeks, Scythians, Parthians, Huns, and Gujars; smothered by the veils of Arabia and Turkistan; and, finally, shamed by the prudery of Victoria. Most of the stories have been taken from the Vedas, Tantras, Itihasas (Ramayana and Mahabharata), and Puranas, as well as from vernacular epics and folk literature held sacred by Hindus. Some have been taken from Hindu scriptures of Bali and Thailand, others from sacred lore of Indian tribes. A few belong to Buddhists and Jains, who share many beliefs with Hindus.

The five faces of the eternal feminine are explored in five chapters. The first chapter forms the foundation of the book as it explores the reaction of the male head to the female body. The next chapter narrates tales in which the woman, the earth, and the mother-goddess are seen as extensions of the same material reality, necessary for existence, hence worthy of reverence and awe. In the third chapter the mother transforms into a nymph, the seductress who offers worldly pleasures and binds man to the cycle of life. The fourth chapter retells the tales of the gradual domestication of women into chaste wives with miraculous powers. In the final chapter the submissive consort redefines herself as the wild and terrifying goddess who does battle, drinks blood, and demands appeasement.

Like all sacred lore, the tales of the Hindus can be seen at various levels. This book considers them primarily from sociological, anthropological, psychological, and philosophical viewpoints. In no way is this book an authoritative, or academic, enterprise. The stories put together are not translations or transliterations; they are summarized retellings. The focus is more on trends than on details.

Each narrative has been churned out of the many versions and variants that exist. The perspective is time-free; five thousand years of history telescope into each tale so that the past and present coalesce. It is almost impossible to organize the tales chronologically. Such is the Hindu way—what was coexists with what is, and what is reflects what will be. Nothing is rejected. Everything is absorbed, sustained, transformed, and celebrated. Shaped by informed interpretation, ornamented with the living imagery of the land, spiced by the flavors of the people, this book delves into the spiral unconscious of the Hindu tradition, rich in ancient memory. It hopes to lift the veil of the Hindu woman a little higher, to reveal expressions rarely seen before.

And while I do so, I gently remind myself that every scripture I have referred to was written by a man in a male-dominated society, every image I have seen was created by a man for male eyes, and I, the author of this book, am male, too. Can I then see the truth about women? Can anyone ever see the truth?

For within infinite myths lies the eternal
  Truth
Who sees it all?
Varuna has but a thousand eyes
Indra has a hundred
And I, only two.

Devdutt Pattanaik
On Holi, 2000

CHAPTER ONE

Left Halves

FEMINIZING THE CIRCLE

Biology and Beyond

She has no face—only a body with a lotus for a head. Images of this faceless woman have been found all over India. They were molded out of clay and carved in rock between the third and the eighth centuries C.E. Knees bent, feet spread apart, breasts and genitals exposed, her characteristic posture is described in the Rig Veda, the oldest and most sacred of Hindu scriptures, as one from which sprang the earth. Known as *uttanapada*, it is the position taken by a woman when she is making love or delivering a child.

Who is this faceless woman? A lover? A mother? A goddess? Nobody knows. Orthodox scriptures offer no explanations. There is no direct reference to such a goddess in the Hindu liturgy. Perhaps the overt sexuality of the image has proved too embarrassing. The embarrassment is evident even in folk explanations for the image:

The great god Shiva was making love to his consort Parvati when sages entered their cave to salute the divine couple. Shiva continued without a pause, much to the disgust of the visitors. They cursed Shiva to be worshipped in the form of a phallus. Embarrassed by the intrusion,

Parvati covered her face with a lotus to be-
come Lajja-gauri, the shy mother-goddess.

Folklore from
the state of Karnataka

Villagers, many of them laborers and serfs who come from the lower strata of the Hindu caste hierarchy, seem more familiar with the icons of Lajja-gauri. They identify her as the primal mother-goddess, the life giver, the life sustainer, the life taker. They call her Adya Shakti (primal energy), Bhudevi (earth-goddess), Renuka (soil maiden), Yellamma (everybody's mother), Sakambari (mother of vegetation), Nagna-Ambika (naked mother). To them, the divinity of the mother-goddess comes from her ability to bring forth life. She is goddess because of her body, not her head.

Fertility, not personality, is what makes woman, earth, and goddess divine. This is re-affirmed by the lotus that replaces the head of Lajja-gauri. The lotus is an ancient fertility symbol representing the power of Nature to draw upon the life force of a bog and trans-form slime into an object of beauty. Goddesses all over the world have been worshipped pri-marily because they are mothers. Biology has always been used to define the woman's role in the secular and sacred scheme of things. Not so for man.

The contribution of male biology to the cycle of life is spasmodic. After he sheds his seed, the chthonian machinery takes over. The womb molds new life; the breasts bloom. The penis lies flaccid, its work done. The male role in Nature's grand plan, though vital, is mo-mentary. The mind ponders: Does man exist only to shed seed?

So while the female body is busy nurtur-ing and nourishing life, the male head ques-tions the purpose of existence. It tries to analyze, understand, and seek meaning in all

Lajja-gauri: Pavarti as the shy mother-goddess.
Stone carving; Panchalingeshvara temple,
Andhra Pradesh.
Late seventh century.

things. It becomes aware that a woman can-not reject her throbbing biology. Her body yokes her to the brute, inflexible rhythm of Nature's procreative law. Every month her body will shed blood and remind her of its potential and purpose. She may not want to have sex, but through love or rape, her body will bear a child. She cannot will her way out of menstruation and pregnancy. Nature claims her body, transforming her into a chthonian tool. Woman must accept her biology. Man does not have to.

Man is the only creature with the potential to oppose Nature's obsession with procreation. Man can choose not to shed his seed in woman. Unlike the bird, the bee, the beast, there is no biological imperative that modulates his sex drive. He can have sex for fun, at will, or not at all. He can resist seduction. If he does not will it, he cannot be forced to shed his seed. His mind can discipline his body not to respond to the biological urge. He has the capacity to challenge the humbling passivity of all creatures to Nature.

Nature is the ultimate authority in the cosmos, winding and unwinding the life force with a rhythmic unconscious regularity, sweeping all creatures to heights of ecstasy before tossing them down to the depths of despair. Nature creates and destroys, inevitably, eventually. Before its awesome power, everyone seems hopelessly helpless. Its impersonality makes the situation worse. So the male mind personified Nature through the female body. Both are beautiful for a purpose, blooming and withering without pause, beyond human control. Both share the life-giving and life-taking vocabulary whose purpose the male head sought to fathom.

The mind rejects the limitations imposed by the body. Imagination does not tolerate subservience to Nature. The male head confronts the female body. Sometimes the mind succumbs, at other times it fights or flees. Flight, fight, freeze— out of this primal reaction to Nature, religion, culture, and civilization came into being.

The mind imagines breaking free from the confines of biology. It conjures up worlds where there is no birth, no death, no change, no suffering. Through mysticism, man hopes to break the fetters that bind him to earth and transcend to the blissful beyond—the realm where man is in charge, a place called heaven.

When flight is impossible, he fights. He explores the mysteries of Nature and uses this knowledge to domesticate and control Nature. He physically suppresses and mentally represses the dark, unwholesome side of Nature. He makes laws that check the dark eroticism of Nature. He builds walls that shut out the ugliness. He writes poetry that mourns the end of good times. Human literature studiously ignores the fact that nothing ever happens in Nature; events keep happening. Man chooses a moment in infinity as the climax of his script and decides whether he wants to celebrate or lament life.

When fight and flight are not possible, man freezes. Feeling helpless, he adores Nature's favorable side and shuns Nature's unfavorable side in the hope that he will experience more of the former and less of the latter. Mother-goddesses come into being; killer-goddesses are appeased or ignored.

Every school of mystical thought, every occult doctrine, every science, every law, every lore is male reaction to the body of female Nature. Every worldview is an attempt to fathom the universe and make life more meaningful.

The Hindu worldview is how the Hindu man perceived life. He saw Nature in the female body. When he adored Nature, he adored woman. When he rejected Nature, he rejected woman. When he exploited Nature, he exploited woman. When he manipulated Nature, he manipulated woman. When he celebrated Nature, he celebrated woman.

The Hindu Worldview

To understand women in sacred Hindu lore, an understanding of the Hindu worldview is vital. In this view life does not begin with birth and does not end with death. Birth and death are alternating events in a relentless journey through the realm of worldly pleasures. This much-desired destination of color, sound, texture, fragrance, and flavor is called *samsara*.

Birth is the acquisition of body and mind that enables one to experience worldly life. Death is the loss of that body and mind. Death is not the end of existence; it is just a transition into a state devoid of sensations but rich in memories that drags one back into the land of the living.

When the body and mind are shed, what remains is the spirit or *atma*. The spirit is everything that the mind and body are not. It is immortal. It is intangible. It has no attributes, hence it cannot be defined. It is the animating principle of the cosmos. It bestows consciousness to a living entity. It is cosmic intelligence that expresses itself through matter.

Matter is energy that flows unconsciously and randomly through the space-time continuum, evolving, dissolving, endlessly transforming. Left alone, matter tends to drift toward entropy—dissolution into a formless, fluid state. Spirit opposes entropy. It rouses the dormant power of matter and transforms it into life-giving energy known as *rasa*. Charged with the spirit, unconscious elements metamorphose into mind and body. Mind and body ensheath the soul, respond to external stimuli, and generate thoughts, feelings, and memories. Thus, living entities that think, feel, and react to samsara come into being.

When the body decays and the mind withers away, the spirit moves on to the land of the dead and waits for another opportunity to unite with matter and return to the land of the living, to think and feel again.

When this opportunity arrives, the qualities of the new mind-body sheath depend on deeds done in the past life. Circumstances surrounding the new mind-body sheath also depend on these deeds. The belief that every event is a reaction to something done in the past is *karma*. Karma rotates the cycle of life.

As long as there are reactions to be experienced, atma is bound to the wheel of existence. Somewhere in this journey, overwhelmed by thoughts and feelings, an ego develops that obstructs the view of the spirit within. This generates restlessness. A quest for meaning begins. Answers are sought in the realm of worldly delights. There is action, reaction, and a fettering of the spirit to samsara. Release comes only with the realization that the true self is not the ego, but the blissful spirit within. Realization occurs only when samsara is witnessed, not reacted to. This is *moksha*.

The spirit realizes itself through mind and body. Mind and body look for the spirit only after confronting the limitations of samsara. Thus, the journey through samsara is the journey of self-realization, a journey from the reality without to the truth within.

The Hindu views life as the opportunity to fulfill karmic obligations (*dharma*), indulge the ego with worldly power (*artha*), gratify the senses with worldly pleasure (*kama*), and discover the spirit (moksha). He can either react to samsara or simply witness it. The former fetters, the latter liberates.

What came first, the key or the lock? When did it all begin? In reply, Hindu seers will ask the inquirer to point to the corner of a circle. When futility of the task is realized, the seers will smile and quote lines from the Rig Veda: "In the beginning, there was neither existence nor nonexistence, neither space nor sky, neither breath nor breathlessness. Who came first? Was it the seed placer or the seed acceptor? Was it desire? Wherefrom? Who knows? Even the gods came later."

Personifying Cosmic Realities

Life is conceived when spirit fuses with matter. At a microcosmic level, birth is observed after a bee visits a blossom, a seed is sown in soil, and a bull mounts a cow. Until the pollen is transmitted, the flower cannot turn into fruit. The soil on its own cannot create a plant. A neglected womb can only shed blood.

Seers, mystics, and alchemists, *rishis*, *yogis*, and *siddhas*, saw within the pollen, the seed, and the semen the spark of life that activates the generative powers of the flower, the soil, and the womb. They felt rasa racing through feminine forms and atma radiant in masculine things. They concluded: Man is the keeper of spirit, and woman, mistress of matter.

Hindu scriptures state, "As is the microcosm, so is the macrocosm; as is the individual body, so is the cosmic body; as is the individual mind, so is the cosmic mind; as is the individual soul, so is the cosmic soul." Bards expanded microcosmic observations to macrocosmic proportions. The earth, like the human body, became a creature alive, a living, breathing entity, going through cycles of life and death, periods of activity and dormancy. Samsara came into being when the cosmic man embraced the cosmic woman:

After the cosmic cataclysm known as pralaya, *all that existed dissolved into the ocean. Nothing existed, neither form nor identity. On the waters that stretched into infinity slept Vishnu in the coils of the serpent of time. At the appointed hour, a lotus rose from his navel and bloomed. Within sat Brahma in serene meditation. Brahma opened his eyes and set about creating the world. He molded sons out of his thoughts. "Go forth and multiply," he told these mind-born sons. But they were passionless seers and could not reproduce. Brahma pondered over the problem and frowned. From his furrowed brow rose Shiva in the form of an androgyne—his right half was male while his left half was female. Inspired by the vision, Brahma split his body and, from the left half, created woman. Her name was Shatarupa. She aroused passion in the hearts of the assembled men. In her body Brahma created offspring who went on to populate the cosmos.*

Vishnu Purana, Shiva Purana

The dissolution of the cosmos into the ocean indicates entropy. Pralaya is the time when the spirit is disembodied. Cosmic intelligence is dormant. Matter is inert. Vishnu sleeps. Then at the appointed hour, cosmic intelligence is roused. The lotus blooms. Brahma, the creator-god who sits on the lotus, seeks to embody the spirit. His mind-born sons lack sexual desire and hence cannot procreate until his body-born daughter comes along and rouses passion.

The association of man with the head, hence rationality, intelligence, and consciousness, and woman with the body, hence intuition, emotion, and carnality, is obvious. Like the ocean, the woman is passive. Like a flower, she is enchanting. When Brahma is enchanted, the seed of life is sown and life renewed. Her opinion is not sought. She is the

Vishnu, symbolizing spirit, with his consort Laxmi, symbolizing matter.
Wall carving; Khajuraho temple, Madhya Pradesh. Twelfth century.

object; he is the subject. She is scenery; he is the seer. She is the primal manifestation. He is the primal cause.

The mind-born sons of Brahma are the *sapta rishis* or the seven cosmic keepers of cosmic intelligence. They are also known as *prajapatis*, lords of progeny, when they use this intelligence to animate matter. The name of Brahma's daughter—Shatarupa, "she-with-many-forms"—indicates that she is the material principle with infinite capacity to transform into any shape or form, depending on information coming from the seers. The theme of spirit-man uniting with matter-woman to create life is elaborated in another story in which Shatarupa multiplies herself into thirteen wives of Kashyapa, a manifestation of Brahma himself:

The mind-born Kashyapa placed his seed in the wombs of his thirteen wives. In due course the women gave birth to different creatures who populate the cosmos. On Aditi, Kashyapa fathered the divine adityas, *on Diti and Danu, the demonic* daityas *and* danavas. *On Kadru, he fathered creatures that crawl like the* nagas; *on Vinata, creatures that fly; on Timi, creatures that swim. On Sarameya, he fathered dogs and wild animals; on Surabhi, cows and tame animals; on Krodhavasa, wild forest spirits such as* rakshasas, yakshas, *and* pisachas. *On Anala, he fathered plants; on Muni, the water-nymphs,* apsaras; *on Aristha, the flower-gods,* gandharvas. *Kashyapa was also father of Manu, the ancestor of mankind. In effect Kashyapa fathered all living creatures. He is therefore known as Prajapati, lord of progeny.*

Bhagvata Purana,
Linga Purana, Kurma Purana

Kashyapa is the mind-born son of Marichi, who is the mind-born son of Brahma. He is not pure passionless spirit; he is spirit that desires embodiment. Until he plants his seed in the thirteen women, nothing happens. When he does plant his seed, thirteen different wombs transform seed from the same source into thirteen different beings. The individuation and differentiation occurs in the wombs. The story successfully captures the essential Hindu philosophy that Nature's variety is merely a material mirage. The wise are not fooled by the apparent differences. They look through cosmic plurality and discover within all creatures the singular divine spirit—the seed of Prajapati.

As bards traveled over hills and across plains, they packaged the Hindu worldview into colorful plots and brought the philosophy of the seer to the common man. But liberties were taken as abstract ideas were concretized and limited by form. Gender was attributed to genderless concepts.

In Samkhya, the oldest school of Hindu metaphysics, the manifested dynamic world comes into being when the restless energies of *prakriti* acquire a direction in the presence of *purusha*, the spirit. Purusha is the unmanifest intelligence that inspires the dance of evolution.

Purusha is the soul of the individual—*jiva-atma*. Vedanta addresses the cosmic soul or *param-atma* as "Brahman" and defines it through negation: *neti-neti*, "not this, not that." It is a transcendental nonentity—neither male nor female, seed nor soil. No form can confine it, no term can describe it. Matter, on the other hand, can be confined by time and space, and can be described variously. Prakriti manifests into both male and female forms. From it come both seed and soil. It is defined through affirmation: *iti-iti*, "this too, that too."

Prakriti throbs with life-bestowing energy or rasa and hence is *shakti*, the source of power. It is also restless and mercurial, hence *maya*, or the stuff of mirage. Brahman, on the other hand, is unchanging and absolute, hence real.

In the colloquial Hindu vocabulary the word *purusha* means "man" while *prakriti* means "Nature." The words *shakti* and *maya* are also expressed in feminine terms. On the tongues of bards the unseen transcendental principle was given a masculine attribute, while the natural world—the world of colors and contours—came to be given a female attribute. A paradigm was created that prejudiced attitudes toward femininity forever. The association of woman with passive matter that is animated and directed by the male spirit did have a profound influence on the gender politics of Hindu society. For it is but a small step from "woman symbolizes Nature" to "woman is Nature."

Ancient Divide

The Hindu worldview, which to most Hindus is *sanatana dharma,* or the eternal truth, was verbalized by seers who realized it after meditating on Vedic verses that were considered too profound to be of human origin. Gender bias is evident even in Vedic verses:

> *Yami approached Yama with love that they might produce children. Yama turned away. "Let Yama behave toward Yami as if she were not his sister. Desire has come upon me. Let me open my body as a wife to a husband. Let us roll like the two wheels of a chariot," she pleaded. "Seek another husband, lovely lady," he said. "Make a pillow of your arm for some bull of man, not me. Never will I unite my body with yours. They call a man who unites with his sister a sinner. Arrange your pleasures with another, not your brother."*

Rig Veda

Yama refuses to touch Yami because she is his sister. He prefers to die childless. With no offspring in the land of the living to facilitate his rebirth, Yama finds himself trapped in the land of the dead, doomed to be the lord of the dead. Yami, without her radiant brother, transforms into Yamini, the mournful lady of the night. In death Yami does not travel to the land of the dead; she remains part of Nature. Yama and others like him in the land of the dead who await rebirth are designated *pitris,* or fathers. Associating spirit with masculinity and Nature with femininity seems like a practice more ancient than human memory.

In some verses of the Rig Veda sky and earth are personified as two goddesses who kiss along the horizon and generate space by their embrace. In this space, on their lap, rides their son, the sun-god, bestowing light, life, and order. Seers invoke the twin goddesses, the mothers, to hold all creatures within samsara and protect them from the dark, shapeless abyss—the realm of death.

The idea of twin goddesses in embrace has led to speculation along the lines of lesbianism among some scholars. The speculation has led to violent debates as to whether homosexual affection is natural or cultural, a universal truism or a Western import.

Some scholars believe that in original hymns natural forces were attributed a neuter gender, and that with the rise of patriarchy divisions appeared to suit patriarchal aspirations: the submissive female below and the dominating male above.

The idea that the male principle is the activating force of the cosmos is widespread in the Vedas. Indra, the sky-god, is described as a great warrior who hurls his thunderbolt against dark clouds and releases waters to help the earth mother bring forth vegetation. The sun is also described as a bull whose virility, transmitted through rays of light, brings forth life. The moon-god's virility, or *soma,* seeps through vegetation and enlivens all things. In other passages the sky is seen as the father who sheds his seed as rain, enabling the earth mother to realize her fertile powers. The

Women in amorous embrace. Wall carving; Khajuraho temple, Madhya Pradesh. Twelfth century.

resulting life is described as rich with butter, sweet with honey, pounding with rasa.

Primal Incest

Yama is mortified by the idea of incest and prefers an eternity in the land of the dead to breaking a moral code. Nature has no moral codes—the womb accepts the semen of father, brother, lover, and rapist. Yami's request to Yama to override intellectual values with biological urges could be seen as yet another attempt to identify women with Nature. "She is more in touch with primal instincts; he is more rational." A modern prejudice with ancient roots.

The idea of primal incest is, however, unavoidable in any creation story. Limited by contemporary values and vocabulary, bards often cringe with embarrassment as they narrate the tale of the one who appeared first in the cycle of life and the one who came second. The second is offspring if born of the first. The second is sibling if born with the first. Either way it is incest. Sacred lore of Indian tribes is full of stories of the first ancestor, who was forced to make his sister his wife because there is no one else around he could make babies with:

Mahadeo created man and woman but they lived separately. So Mahadeo took the form of ants, scorpions, and snakes and scared the woman to take refuge in the arms of the man. Though together, the first man and the first woman did not know how to make love; so Mahadeo taught them the art of tickling, which aroused passion and enabled them to have intercourse.

Tribal lore from the state of Orissa

Human values come second to Nature's demand. In the Rig Veda the goddess of dawn, called Ushas, recoils in horror because she is penetrated by her father, but nevertheless gives in for the sake of natural order. She is praised for this. In the Brahmanas, ritual manuals based on Vedic hymns, Prajapati takes up the role of creation and Rudra punishes him for his incestuous desire. While the act is condemned, the fruit of incest is not:

Prajapati created sons by the power of his mind. But these could not multiply. So he created the woman Sandhya, who was dawn itself. She was so beautiful that Prajapati, overwhelmed with desire, tried to embrace her. Sandhya ran to the sky. Prajapati followed her. "The father is doing what is not to be done," cried Brahma's sons. They called upon Rudra, the howler, to punish their father. He shot an arrow and injured

Prajapati, whose seed fell to form a lake. "Let the seed not be wasted," said his sons. Out of it came the animals.

Aitareya Brahmana

In the Puranas—texts that play an immediate role in modern Hinduism, as compared with the Vedas and Brahmanas—Prajapati is identified with Brahma and Rudra with Shiva, the god of destruction. Brahma must have sex with his daughter, even it means he becomes unworthy of Hindu worship, with no temple or festival in his honor:

Sandhya, disgusted by her father's deed, propitiated Shiva and asked that all newborns should be free from desire and incapable of arousing lust. Shiva cursed Brahma that there would be no temples or festivals in his honor.

Shiva Purana

Brahma is creator in the *margi*, or classical Hindu tradition. In the *desi*, or folk traditions, the creator is a goddess. She makes the decisions and must contend with the consequences of incestuous desire as she goes about creating the world:

Before there were hills, fields, and plants, there was only water. From this water came Adya, born to herself. The moment she was born, she grew to womanhood and the desire for man arose within her. In the form of a bird she sat on the lotus and laid three eggs. The first egg was spoilt. From the second came the sky, the sun, the moon, the stars, and the encircling sea. From the third

came the gods Brahma, Vishnu, and Shiva. *Adya nurtured the three gods on her bosom, and they grew up to be virile youths. Then, adorning herself with jewels and flowers, she asked the gods to unite with her. Brahma and Vishnu were horrified by the idea, for she was their mother; but Shiva agreed provided she gave him her third eye. Overwhelmed by desire, Adya gave her third eye and instantly lost her radiance and became an old woman, gaunt with wrinkled skin and shriveled breasts. The gods became powerful and set about creating, preserving, and destroying the universe. With desire went youth. The ancient goddess remained to fight and kill demons and drink their blood.*

Folklore from the
state of Andhra Pradesh

This tale of Adya has led to speculations that the Indian hinterland retains a memory of the time when the cult of the mother-goddess was overtaken by male-dominated orders. One story from the ancient margi scripture probably does record the overthrow of an ancient, fertile, seed-seeking earth-goddess:

A woman with a long tongue was licking away soma, *the sacred sacrificial oblation meant for the gods. The devas did not want to share the* soma, *the source of their divine splendor, with anyone. They had killed their half-brothers, the asuras, for much less. Deeming Dirghajihvi, the long-tongued woman, to be an ogress, the gods plotted to kill her. First they stopped all sacrifices so that no more soma was produced. Then Indra, leader of the devas, tried to grab her. He failed. So he recruited the handsome Sumitra to seduce and overpower her. "Women like to flirt with a good-looking man,"*

Indra said. Sumitra, however, failed in his mission. Dirghajihvi's body was covered with vaginas, and Sumitra's single penis could not satisfy her. Indra then caused Sumitra to sprout several penises all over his body and sent him back to Dirghjihvi. This time Sumitra succeeded. He mounted Dirghajihvi and, having entered her, refused to leave. "Let go," she cried, "I thought you were a good friend." "I am a good friend to good friends and a bad friend to bad friends," replied Sumitra, pinning Dirghajihvi down. He then summoned Indra, who hurled his thunderbolt and killed Dirghajihvi.

Jaiminiya Brahmana

The truth may never be known. As one ponders over who came first, man or woman, and wonders who is the creator and who the creation, one must cast one's eyes on a rather interesting line from the Rig Veda: "From Aditi, the unfettered mother, was born Daksha, the dextrous father. From Daksha, the dextrous father, was born Aditi, the unfettered mother."

Male Spirit and Female Matter

Though Vedic ideas dominate Hindu thought, Hinduism is an amalgam of many diverse ideas, from Vedantic speculation to Yogic mysticism, Tantrik alchemy to Brahmanical ritualism. In addition, Hinduism embraced, imbibed, and enriched itself with innumerable folk beliefs and tribal customs. These percolated into Vedic society over several centuries, giving rise to modern-day Hinduism.

In Vedic rituals known as *yagnas* seers sought to empower celestial beings with oblations and chants in the hope that they would maintain a steady flow of life-bestowing rasa into human society. With the passage of time, these elaborate ceremonies no longer satisfied the spiritual needs of society. Some turned to monastic orders such as Buddhism and Jainism. Others turned to mystical practices such as *yoga*. Many turned to theism and ecstatic devotion known as *bhakti*. Through rites of adoration known as *pujas*, devotees sought to propitiate almighty beings who were held responsible for the cycle of life.

Some personified the supreme divine principle as Shiva, the world-rejecting ascetic, while others personified it as Vishnu, the world-appreciating warrior, especially in the most charming of his incarnations—Krishna.

Shiva and Vishnu, the two pillars of Hindu theism, were not worshipped in isolation. Each had a consort: Shiva had Shakti; Vishnu had Laxmi. It was believed that the gods were powerless without their consorts. They were shaktis, fountainheads of power and radiance. Only in the womb of the goddesses could the gods manifest themselves.

For devotees of Shiva, the manhood, or *lingam*, of the god contains the seed of cosmic consciousness, while the womb, or *yoni*, of the goddess is the space-time vessel of all energies. The world exists so long as the two are united. Separation means cosmic dissolution:

womb to capture and contain Shiva's lingam. Within Shakti's yoni the fearsome energy of Shiva's lingam was dissipated. Thus the union of Shiva and Shakti saved the world from destruction. The image of Shiva's lingam locked in Shakti's yoni is therefore revered by all.

Shiva Purana

The name Shiva means "purity." As pure consciousness, Shiva is untainted by all obligations, actions, and forms. In the above story Shiva is unconcerned about the loss of his manhood. He seems almost indifferent to the resulting chaos. Shiva's reluctance to marry is a consistent theme in Shaiva lore. In effect he opposes the birth of the cosmos, preferring the blissful state in which matter is in a state of entropy and the spirit is free of form. Not surprisingly, he is called the god of destruction.

Vishnu is the god who sustains and maintains what Brahma creates and what Shiva seeks to destroy. He is also pure consciousness. His name means "pervader." Vishnu pervades and enlivens all things. For devotees of Vishnu, Vishnu's blue color indicates that he is as pervasive and intangible as the sky, while his consort Laxmi's red sari represents earth's all-containing fertility. He is the protector; she is the provider:

✳

The sages were angry to find Shiva wandering through their hermitage, naked with penis erect. So they castrated him. Shiva's penis then turned into a fiery missile and moved in every direction, threatening to destroy the three worlds. The sages propitiated Brahma, who told them that unless Shiva's lingam was brought to rest it would destroy the cosmos. So the sages invoked Shakti, who offered her

✳

The earth-goddess Bhudevi, who is Laxmi, floated on the sea, lapped by the waves, warmed by the sun, moistened by rain. One day the demon Hiranyaksha dragged Bhudevi under the sea. As she cried for help, Vishnu took the form of a wild boar, plunged into the sea, gored Hiranyaksha to death, and saved the earth-goddess. As they rose to the surface, Vishnu embraced Bhudevi

Vishnu, in the form of a boar, lifting the earth-goddess from the bottom of the sea.
Stone carving from the queen's stepwell of Patan, Gujarat. Eleventh century.

passionately. Thus hills and valleys came into being. He plunged his virile tusks into the soil and impregnated the earth-goddess with seed. Thus plants and trees were born. Bhudevi accepted Vishnu as her guardian and named him Bhupati, lord of the earth. As the blue sky, Vishnu promised to watch over her at all times.

Bhagvata Purana

In popular versions of sacred Hindu lore a male trinity rotates the wheel of life. Brahma creates. Vishnu sustains. Shiva destroys. To cre-ate, Brahma needs information that comes from Sarasvati, goddess of knowledge, his consort. To sustain, Vishnu needs wherewithal, which is provided by his consort Laxmi, goddess of wealth and power. Shiva becomes the destroyer, ac-quiring strength and inspiration from his con-sort Shakti, who is both Gauri, radiant goddess of eroticism, and Kali, dark goddess of extermi-nation. The gods are deciding and doing; the goddesses simply are. Sarasvati personifies Nature's wisdom. Laxmi personifies Nature's bounty. Shakti personifies Nature's power to spontaneously and simultaneously bring forth and consume life. The goddesses passively make up the wheel of existence that the gods react to and actively rotate.

Left and Right Halves of the Whole

Matter and soul, like woman and man, complement each other. He is the potter, she is clay. The pot of life needs both. Hindu bards have imaginatively captured this interdepen-

dence by presenting the two realities as two halves of one body:

✳

The sage Bhringi wanted to circumambulate Shiva. The goddess Parvati stopped him. "You must go around both of us because he is incomplete without me." But the sage refused to go around her. So Parvati embraced her lord and made it impossible for Bhringi to go around Shiva alone. Determined to

Ardhanari, the god Shiva whose left half is feminine.
Patta painting, folk style from Orissa. Twentieth century.

salute only Shiva, Bhringi decided to take the form of a bee and fly around Shiva's top-knot. To thwart his plans, Parvati fused her body with Shiva so that they became two halves of a singular being—she formed the left half, he the right. Bhringi then decided to take the form of a worm, bore a path between the two halves of the divine androgyne, and go only around the right half. Enraged by Bhringi's persistence, the goddess caused the sage's two legs to become so weak that he could not stand or move. Bhringi begged for mercy. Only when he agreed to go around both the god and the goddess was he given a third leg that enabled him to stand and hobble around the divine couple.

Temple tale from Tamil Nadu

By attempting to ignore the goddess who is energy, Bhringi loses the power to move. Without her, even Shiva is but a corpse, a *shava*.

Parvati makes up the left half of the androgyne. Shatarupa emerges from the left half of Brahma. The association of femininity with the left half is so strong in Hindu beliefs that woman is described as *vamangi*, "beautiful-one-on-the-left." Fertility cults that give women prominence, such as Tantra, are designated *vamachari*, "left-handed paths." In Hindu ceremonies a woman always sits to the left of the husband. In temples the idol of the goddess is always placed to the left of the god. Why left? There are no clear answers. In this context one comes across a rather interesting story in the epic Mahabharata:

Ganga, the river-goddess, saw Pratipa, king of Hastinapur, meditating on the banks of the river. She went and sat on his lap and asked him to marry her. The king refused, as he had renounced the world. When Ganga persisted, Pratipa said, "Had you sat on my left thigh, I would have considered you my wife. You sat on my right thigh, which is reserved for daughters. So go and marry my son Shantanu, for I can look upon you only as my daughter-in-law."

Mahabharata

It could be that with the wife on the left side, the right hand was free for the warrior to wield his sword and the priest to offer oblations. It also could be that the left side of the body is where the heart is located—and since the heart is the seat of all emotions and instincts, that is where Mother Nature was placed. Or the ancients may have placed man on the right because they knew that the right half of the body is controlled by the left brain, which modern science confirms is the seat of logic. It must also be noted that the left half is considered impure and inauspicious in Hinduism. Gifts are never offered with or received in the left hand. Food is never picked up with the left hand. The left hand is reserved to clean the body after ablutions. One can only wonder what this says about the Hindu attitude toward womanhood.

CHAPTER TWO

Earth Mother

ROTATING THE CIRCLE

Cycle of Fertility

In sacred Hindu lore goddess, earth, and woman are perceived as extensions of the same material reality. Their creative energy, rasa, ebbs and flows as devas battle their eternal enemies, the asuras. When devas win, the goddess smiles; earth and women are ready to receive seed. When they lose, asuras sap rasa, the goddess frowns, the fields dry up, and women menstruate. The resulting cycle of fertility is known as *ritu*.

To support devas and harness the benevolent energies of Nature, a magical draft known as soma was prepared during Vedic yagnas. This soma was the earthly counterpart of *amrita*, nectar of immortality, that had transformed devas long ago into gods of light, life, and order:

The adityas, sons of Brahma by Aditi, sought to churn out amrita from the ocean of milk. The enterprise required the cooperation of their eternal enemies, the daityas, sons of Brahma by Diti. Meru, the axis of space, was used as the spindle and Adi-Anata-Sesha, the serpent of time, served as the rope of the cosmic churn. Akupara, the turtle who supports the universe on his back, served as the base of the churn and prevented Meru from sinking. The two

sets of divine spirits acted as the force and the counterforce. When the nectar of immortality emerged, Vishnu, the champion of the adityas, took the form of the enchantress Mohini, bewitched the daityas with looks of passion, and poured every drop of amrita down the throats of the adityas. Thus the adityas became devas, immortal keepers of fertility. Deprived of the drink, the daityas remained asuras, "demons who were denied nectar." The devas drove the asuras into the netherworld, claimed the magnificent gifts that emerged from the sea, and rose to the celestial spheres known as svarga, *where they built the fabulous city of Amravati.*

Mahabharata, Ramayana

The ocean of milk is matter in a state of entropy. The devas agitate its still waters and draw out gifts that transforms svarga into a realm of eternal life and endless joy. Man may not have eternity, but he does have a lifetime to enjoy the wonders of samsara. Earth is his ocean of milk. By tilling it, he can churn out all that he desires. But to enjoy it, he needs woman.

Pots of Immortality and Baskets of Bounty

Woman gives man access to samsara. Through her womb the dead return to the land of the living. In her arms man finds pleasure. In pleasure he acquires family and becomes lord of the household. Family responsibilities give man the moral right to own property and wield power. A wife is the key to worldly pleasure, kama, and worldly power, artha. She is therefore referred to as Griha-Laxmi, the household goddess of fortune, a diminutive double of

Maha-Laxmi, the cosmic goddess of fortune, who gave devas all that they desired when she emerged from the ocean of milk:

As the gods and demons churned the ocean of milk, rasa coagulated and began to take wonderful shapes. Laxmi, the goddess of abundance and affluence, emerged dressed in red, bedecked in gold, seated on a thousand-petaled dew-drenched lotus. Dhanavantari, the god of health, stood beside her holding a pot containing the nectar of immortality, amrita. To enjoy the eternal life guaranteed by amrita, the goddess brought along many magnificent gifts. There were gifts that guaranteed prosperity—Kamadhenu, the cow whose udders were always filled with milk; Kalpataru, the tree whose branches were always laden with fruit; Chintamani, the priceless wish-fulfilling gem. There were gifts offering pleasure—Chandra, the handsome moon-god; Rambha, a ravishing nymph well versed in the erotic arts; Varuni, the goddess of wine. There were also gifts of power—Airavata, the six-tusked white-skinned royal elephant; Ucchaishrava, the virile seven-headed battle horse that always broke through enemy lines; Saranga, the bow that never missed its target; Panchajanya, the conch-trumpet that scared away rivals. With these gifts, the goddess brought worldly joy into the wheel of existence.

Padma Purana,
Bhagvata Purana, Laxmi Tantra

The tale of Laxmi's emergence from the ocean is an integral part of the Hindu narrative tradition. It is found in almost every sacred book and is recounted during wedding ceremonies. By capturing the Hindu vision of

The gods and demons churning Laxmi, the goddess of wealth and fortune, out of the ocean of milk.
Karnataka painting; popular craft from Mysore. Twentieth century.

paradise—where there is eternal health, wealth, power, and pleasure—it suppresses the fear of death, change, and hopelessness. For the death-fearing celestial beings, the goddess Laxmi offers what a woman, at a microcosmic level, is believed to bring into a household—the promise and pleasure of worldly life.

Without a woman, according to Hindu scriptures, a man can only be a *brahmachari*, a chaste student, or a *sanyasi*, a celibate hermit. Without a woman by his side, a man is forbidden from performing yagnas. Only when he is a *grihastha*, or householder, do gods accept his gifts and bestow him favor. The wife is *sowbhagyavati*, "bearer of good fortune." She is like the goddess whose absence creates havoc in the heavens:

Rambha offered the sage Durvasa a garland of celestial flowers. Durvasa decided to give it to Indra, king of the devas. Indra was too drunk to appreciate the gift. He placed the garland on the trunk of his elephant Airavata. Airavata threw it on the floor.

Ucchaishrava, the seven-headed horse of Indra, walked over it. Infuriated, Durvasa cursed Indra that he would lose Laxmi's favor. Instantly, the goddess returned to the ocean of milk. Kalpataru withered. Kamadhenu refused to shed milk. Chintamani lost its luster. To win her back, the devas had to once more churn the ocean of milk.

Brahmavaivarta Purana

When a new bride steps into her husband's house for the first time, dressed in red, bedecked with flowers, jewels, and sixteen love charms, conches are blown and grains of rice sprinkled. With her comes the happiness of the present generation and hope of the next.

Debt to Ancestors

Man incurs a debt as soon as he enters samsara. He owes his existence to his pitris, or forefathers. He must therefore produce offspring and facilitate their reentry into the land of the living. In annual *shradha* ceremonies men make offerings of rice balls to pitris and reaffirm the promise to fulfill their biological obligation. The rice balls, or *pindas,* are eaten by crows that, it is said, carry messages to the land of ancestors.

When a man refuses to have anything to do with women, pitris are annoyed. They appear in his dreams and torment him with visions of their suffering until he concedes to their wishes:

One night, the hermit Jaratkaru saw a vision. He saw his forefathers suspended by

their heels over a dark abyss. "What can I do to save you?" he asked. "Father sons that we may be reborn," said the ancestors. Jaratkaru was thus forced to marry and fulfill his biological obligation to his ancestors.

Mahabharata

Because the spirit of ancestors lies locked in the male seed, semen is too precious a body fluid to be wasted. This is one of the many reasons why masturbation is frowned upon in Hinduism:

Uparichara was resting in the forest after a hunt when desire came upon him and he shed his semen on the forest floor. Not wanting to waste it, he wrapped it in a leaf and instructed a parrot to carry it to his beloved wife in the palace that she may place it in her ripe womb.

Mahabharata

Ancestors never appear in a woman's dream. Although women also owe their existence to forefathers, the debt to ancestors falls squarely on male shoulders. For in the rite of conception, the man performs. A woman merely presents herself. If she does not, she does not gain entry into heaven:

The daughter of sage Kunigarga performed austerities and refused any contact with men. Though she conquered her senses she was not allowed to enter heaven, because she had not performed her worldly duties. When she returned to earth no man would marry her, as she was old and ugly. So she offered half the merits of her austerities to

*any man who would marry her. The sage
Shringavan accepted her offer, married her,
and made love to her for one night. The next
day she abandoned her body and discovered
she could enter heaven.*

Mahabharata

A wife rescues her husband from the wrath
of pitris. Without her support, he is doomed
to rot in the hell called *put* reserved for childless men. In the following story the wife practices necrophilia to save her husband from
such a terrible fate:

*King Vyushtiashva died before he could bear
any children. His heartbroken widow, Bhadra,
did not let his corpse be cremated. She clung to
her husband's dead body day and night and
mourned her inability to help him repay his debt
to his ancestors. Feeling sorry for her, the gods
advised her to lie next to the corpse during her
fertile period. Bhadra did as she was told and
went on to bear the dead king several illustrious sons.*

Mahabharata

The wife is a man's shakti. She enriches
his life. She empowers him to repay his debt
to his ancestors. In the microcosm of the
household she is the goddess, and he is the
god. He sheds his role as Shiva, unites with
her as Brahma, and then raises the child as
Vishnu.

Gift of a Daughter

Sages, after being confronted with the vision
of suffering pitris, went to kings and sought

their daughters in marriage. In ancient Hindu
society, kings were obliged to take care of the
worldly needs of hermits. Giving a daughter
to a sage or priest who served a king was considered the way of the devas or gods:

*The sage Agastya saw his ancestors on the
verge of falling into a dark chasm. To save
them, Agastya decided to marry. He went
to the king of Vidharba, but the king was
reluctant to give his daughter Lopamudra to
an ascetic. Realizing her father's predicament, Lopamudra herself asked to be given
to Agastya. She discarded her royal robes
and followed the hermit to the forest.*

Mahabharata

The gift of a girl, or *kanya-dan*, earned great
merit because it was the gift of life. A household without a girl-child was considered incomplete and unfortunate:

*For two years the child in Gandhari's womb
showed no signs of coming out. When
Gandhari learned that her sister-in-law
Kunti, who had become pregnant after her,
had already delivered a son, she refused to
wait any longer. She ordered her maid to
strike her stomach with an iron bar. Out
came a ball of flesh, hard and cold as metal.
Gandhari sent for the sage Vyasa, who had
foretold she would be mother of a hundred
sons, and demanded an explanation. Vyasa
asked the maid to get a hundred pots of clarified butter. He cut the ball of flesh into tiny
pieces and put one piece in each of the pots.
After nine months, the pots were broken and
Gandhari found a male child in all of them.*

Thus did Gandhari become mother of a hundred sons. Gandhari, however, longed to nurse a female child. Vyasa read her mind. He had saved one piece of the ball of flesh. Chanting a magic formula, he incubated that piece of flesh in a pot of butter until it turned into a girl-child. Thus was born Gandhari's daughter, who was named Dushala.

Mahabharata

While giving away daughters, fathers were concerned about their daughters' welfare:

King Mandhata had fifty daughters. An old but powerful sage called Saubhari asked for one of them in marriage. Unwilling to give away any of his young daughters to this old man, yet afraid to refuse, Mandhata said that the choice should be left to the girls. Divining the king's discomfort, Saubhari used his powers and transformed himself into an attractive young man. All fifty princesses fell in love with him and wished to be his wife. Saubhari married them all. He then split himself into fifty vigorous husbands and satisfied all fifty princesses, each one believing that he was devoted to her exclusively.

Padma Purana, Vishnu Purana

A father often wondered if the man who married his daughter was strong enough to protect her. Many fathers therefore organized martial competitions and gave their daughters to the champion:

Nagnajit, king of Kosala, invited warriors from all over the land to tame seven of his wildest bulls and win his daughter Satya's

hand in marriage. Kings came, tried, and failed. Finally, Krishna, scion of the Yadava clan, entered the ring. He multiplied his body seven times. With each form, he grabbed a bull by the horns and forced it into submission. Krishna then tied the seven bulls with a rope and dragged them toward Nagnajit as if they were seven toy bulls. Pleased with this display of courage and strength, Nagnajit was more than happy to let Satya marry Krishna.

Bhagvata Purana

Some fathers gave their daughters away to men who defeated them in battle. This was not just a peace offering. The victor was viewed as a stronger man and hence more capable of protecting the daughter:

Krishna went to the forest looking for the Syamantaka gem and traced it to the cave of Jambavan, king of bears. Jambavan refused to part with it without a fight. In the duel that followed, Krishna defeated Jambavan and claimed the gem. Impressed by Krishna's skill and strength in hand-to-hand combat, Jambavan gave Krishna his daughter Jambhavati's hand in marriage.

Bhagvata Purana

Sometimes the suitors fought among themselves and the winner of the war took home the bride:

Everyone wanted to marry the princess Balandhara of Kashi. Her father decided that the one who could triumph over all other suitors had the right to marry her. Bhima,

A princess garlanding (marrying) a prince who wins her hand by triumphing in a martial contest. Madhubani painting; popular style from Bihar. Twentieth century.

the Pandava, rose to the challenge, fought and defeated all the warriors who had assembled at Kashi. He then took Balandhara as his bride. No one dared stop him.

Mahabharata

Fathers also checked the character of a man before making him son-in-law. Nothing was worse than giving the daughter to a man of loose morals:

The sage Vadanya refused to let Ashtavakra marry his daughter Suprabha until he had paid a visit to the abode of damsels, stri-rajya, and spoken to its ruler, the beautiful Uttara. When Ashtavakra reached the abode of damsels, located to the north of the Himalayas, Uttara welcomed him enthusiastically. She spoke at length on subjects ranging from love to erotica. When Ashtavakra prepared to leave, she begged him to stay back and marry her. She offered him physical pleasures that were beyond human imagination. Ashtavakra refused, as his heart belonged to Suprabha. Instead of getting angry, Uttara smiled. She revealed that she had been asked by Vadanya to test his resolve. She blessed

Ashtavakra and wished him a happy married life.

Mahabharata

Fathers always sought a man with many noble qualities as son-in-law. To entice him into marriage, they offered him a dowry and bedecked the bride with expensive clothes and jewelry. *Brahmanas*, or members of the priestly class, who were highly educated but were forbidden from possessing worldly wealth, preferred this method of marriage. Hence, this form of marriage was called *brahmya-vivah*. It became the preferred form of marriage in Hindu society:

After Krishna, the cowherd, killed Kamsa, the king of the Yadavas, the secret of his birth was revealed to all. He was in fact the son of Kamsa's sister Devaki, who was raised in secret among low-caste cowherds to protect him from his uncle whose nemesis he was destined to be. Though he was ritually purified, educated, and welcomed into the royal fold, many doubted his royal roots. In Dwarka lived a Yadava called Satrajit who possessed a magical gem called Syamantaka that bestowed its owner with good fortune. Krishna admired this gem and advised Satrajit to give it to the Yadava people. Satrajit refused to part with it. He gave it instead to his brother Prasena, who wore it around his neck and went out hunting. Not long after, Prasena was found dead in the forest, his body mauled by a lion. The gem could not be found anywhere near the corpse. Everyone jumped to the conclusion that Krishna had stolen the gem. To clear his name, Krishna went to the forest and traced the gem to the cave of the bear-king

Jambavan, who had found the sparkling stone near the corpse and brought it home for his sons to play with. Krishna restored the stone to Satrajit. Impressed with Krishna's strength of character, Satrajit had Krishna married to his daughter Satyabhama. She came into Krishna's house with a dowry that made her the richest woman in Dwarka. Satrajit also gave Krishna the Syamantaka gem, but Krishna refused to take it. Satyabhama's suitors were so upset to learn of her marriage to Krishna that they murdered Satrajit and stole the Syamantaka. Krishna found the murderers and restored the gem to the Yadava people.

Bhagvata Purana

The wealth that came with the wife belonged to her alone and so was known as *stridhan*. Sacred Hindu lore abounds with tales of Satyabhama showing off her wealth to spite Krishna's other wife, Rukmini, who was extremely poor; she had eloped with Krishna with no gifts from her father's house:

Narada once came to Krishna's palace for alms. Krishna's queens offered him anything he wished. "I want Krishna," he said. Horrified by this request, Krishna's eight wives asked Narada to ask for anything else but Krishna. "Give me something worth Krishna in weight," said the sage. So the queens made Krishna sit on one pan of a balance and wondered what they could put on the other pan that was as heavy as Krishna. Some queens brought fruits, others brought books—but nothing seemed to balance Krishna's weight. Satyabhama ordered her servants to bring all her jewelry. Even that could not balance Krishna's weight. Finally,

Rukmini placed on the pan a sprig of the tulsi plant, saying, "This symbolizes my love for Krishna." Instantly, the balance tilted in Rukmini's favor. Her love was worth much more than Satyabhama's gold.

Folklore from the state of Orissa

Love of a Woman

Not every woman agreed to marry the man her father chose. Women were ready to elope with the man of their dreams:

Rukmi, prince of Vidharba, had fixed his sister Rukmini's marriage with Sishupala, king of Chedi. Rukmini wanted to marry Krishna, lord of Dwarka. She sent a secret message to Dwarka and begged Krishna to come to her rescue. On the wedding day, as she was about to enter the marriage pavilion after visiting the shrine of the mother-goddess, Krishna rode into her city on a golden chariot and whisked her away.

Bhagvata Purana

Sacred texts have always given more importance to a woman's love than a father's wish. Indeed, the greatest love story in sacred Hindu lore is the adulterous love of Radha for Krishna while he lived among cowherds long before he went to Dwarka and married Rukmini. This was considered pure love, beyond all social confines, hence divine:

Radha was married to Rayana, brother of Yashoda, Krishna's foster mother. But she was in love with Krishna. Every night she would slip out of her house in the middle of the night, risk her reputation, and visit Krishna on the banks of the River Yamuna. Together, they would dance and make love in flowery meadows. Soon everybody was talking about the scandalous relationship. Radha was ostracized by all. Krishna took ill. His body burnt with a mysterious fever. The cowherds blamed Radha for it. None of the village doctors could cure Krishna, so Yashoda sent for a great sage who lived in the forest nearby. The sage said that water carried in a sieve would cure Krishna. "How could that be done?" asked the cowherds. "By the powers of chastity," explained the sage. So every woman in the village was asked to fetch water in a sieve. Not a single woman succeeded. Finally, it was Radha's turn. She brought water in a sieve to Krishna as if she were carrying it in a metal pot. The whole village realized that Radha's love was unconditional, hence her relationship with Krishna chaste.

Folklore from the state of Uttar Pradesh

The best way to get a wife was to win her heart. This method was taken up by many Hindu high gods like Shiva and Vishnu to marry village goddesses. In the following story Shiva's son, the virile warrior-god Kartikeya, worshipped by Tamils as Murugan, secures a wife for himself from among the hill tribes:

A tribal chief discovered Valli near an anthill and, realizing she was of divine origin, raised her as his daughter. Valli often took care of her father's millet fields. One day Murugan saw her and fell in love. He tried to charm her with amorous words, but she

turned away from him. He took the form of a bangle seller, then a sage, and tried to endear himself to her. But she drove him away. Finally, Murugan asked his elephant-headed brother, Ganesha, to come to his aid. Ganesha took the form of a wild elephant and rushed into the field. To save herself, Valli ran straight into Murugan's arms. Murugan drove the elephant away and won Valli's heart. Her father opposed their wedding. But Murugan fought him and his sons with his lance. Impressed by his valor, they accepted him as son-in-law of the tribe.

Folklore from the
state of Tamil Nadu

In Tamil Nadu and Andhra Pradesh many villages have temples dedicated to Vishnu, whose consort is the local manifestation of Vishnu's consort, Laxmi:

The sage Bhrigu kicked Vishnu on his chest because Vishnu had not risen to greet him. Laxmi, Vishnu's consort, who resided on Vishnu's chest, was furious when she found Vishnu apologizing to Bhrigu instead of punishing him for hurting her. In her wrath she left the heavens and descended upon earth to the city of Kolhapur. Vishnu followed her but, finding her unwilling to return, sought shelter in the hills of Vyenkata until she calmed down. One day, while chasing a wild elephant, he saw a beautiful maiden in a garden. Her name was Padmavati, "lotus girl." She had been ploughed out of earth by a local king who recognized her as a manifestation of the earth-goddess. Vishnu wished to marry her. At first she rejected his advances. With strength and charm, Vishnu managed to change her mind. But there was a bridal price to pay and with-

out the goddess of wealth Laxmi by his side, Vishnu was a pauper. He was forced to take a loan and thus became indebted to the goddess forever.

Tirumala Sthala Purana
from the state of Andhra Pradesh

In another village the story of Vishnu's serial marriages to local goddesses continues:

On learning of Vishnu's marriage to Padmavati, the goddess Laxmi was furious. So she took birth in a lotus in a village nearby. The sage Bhrigu discovered her and raised her as his daughter. This was his way of making amends for kicking Vishnu on his chest. He named her Kamalavali, "lotus one." Kamalavali grew up to be a very beautiful girl. One day, as she sat under a coral tree, Vishnu passed the village on a chariot. Struck by her beauty, he decided to marry her and settle down in that village.

Kamalavali Sthala Purana,
from the state of Andhra Pradesh

These tales hold the secret of how classical Shaiva and Vaishnava traditions merged with goddess-dominated folk traditions and spread across the land. There is a mixture of love and force. It is interesting to note that in many villages the shrine of the goddess is usually separate from the husband. The goddess thus retains her autonomy. The reason given for the separate shrines is usually an altercation over a petty issue, such as Vishnu going out of the house without the goddess's permission. The annual reconciliation and union is a village festival.

Choosing Husbands

A woman's desire was considered more important than the wishes of her kinsmen. In ancient India women had the right to choose their own husbands. One woman traveled all over the world looking for a husband worthy of her:

Savitri, daughter of the king Ashvapati, was so beautiful and intelligent that men shied away from asking her hand in marriage. So Savitri decided to travel to every kingdom in the land and look for a suitable groom for herself. As she rode through the forest, she met a woodcutter called Satyavan. His father was a king who had been driven out of his kingdom by his enemies. Savitri informed her father of her desire to marry Satyavan. Ashvapati was not pleased. Not only was Satyavan poor; oracles also predicted that he would die within a year of marriage. When Ashvapati saw that his daughter was determined to marry the man of her choice, he gave his consent and made arrangements for the wedding.

Mahabharata

Even the gods helped women find husbands of their choice:

Daityasena and Devasena were two daughters of Daksha who were amusing themselves in a lake when the demon Kini came upon them. Aroused by their beauty, he sought both their hands in marriage. Daityasena agreed to marry him. When Devasena refused, Kini tried to use force. Indra, who heard *Devasena's cries for help, hurled his thunderbolt and frightened Kini into the nether regions. Indra heard Devasena's desire to marry a man who could single-handedly defeat the demons. There was only one god who could do this. His name was Kartikeya, son of Shiva, commander of the celestial armies. Kartikeya married Devasena, adopted daughter of Indra, who assisted him whenever he rode into battle.*

Mahabharata

Incidentally, the names Daityasena and Devasena mean "army of the demons" and "army of the gods," respectively. Thus the two women personify armies, the shakti of the celestial beings, who choose whom they wish to serve.

The demand for women was so great that men often gathered in a woman's house to help her choose a groom. This self-choice ceremony was known as *swayamvara*:

The two sages Narada and Parvata fell in love with the princess Srimati. Each went secretly to her father and sought her hand in marriage but were curtly told that she would choose her husband by herself. Then each one went to Vishnu and asked him to give his rival a monkey face. Each sage went to Srimati's self-choice ceremony thinking that the other had a monkey face. Repulsed by both their monkey faces, the princess garlanded a handsome youth instead. The youth turned out to be Vishnu in disguise.

Linga Purana

To help a woman make up her mind, men were invited to participate in a test of skill organized by the father:

King Drupada organized an archery contest. Warriors and princes were invited to string a stiff bow, then shoot the eye of a fish rotating on a wheel hanging from the roof by looking at its reflection in a pond below. He who succeeded, it was announced, would marry the king's beautiful daughter Draupadi.

Mahabharata

If a man did not meet with a woman's approval, she could stop him from participating in the competition:

Karna, king of Anga, decided to participate in the archery competition organized by Drupada. However, when he strung the bow, the king's daughter stopped him from proceeding further. "I do not wish to marry a man who does not know who his parents are and who was raised in the family of lowly charioteers."

Mahabharata

When a woman chose her own lover and married without seeking family consent, she was said to be following the way of the flower-gods known as gandharvas:

Usha, daughter of King Bana, saw the face of Aniruddha in her dreams. Determined to marry this prince of Dwarka, she sent the witch Chitralekha to abduct him and bring him to her. Chitralekha flew into the city of Dwarka in the middle of the night, picked up Aniruddha as he lay asleep, and carried him to Usha's bedchamber. When Anirud-

dha woke up, he was pleasantly surprised to find himself in the arms of a beautiful woman. Usha's father, Bana, was not pleased to see Aniruddha with his daughter, because Aniruddha's grandfather Krishna was his sworn enemy. He had Aniruddha thrown into prison. Krishna immediately rushed to his grandson's rescue. In the battle that followed, Krishna killed Bana and installed Usha on the throne with Aniruddha as her consort.

Bhagvata Purana

One woman was so determined to marry the man of her choice that she even approved his killing of her brother:

Hidimba, a man-eating rakshasa, sent his sister Hidimbi to kill the five Pandava princes and their mother, who were traveling through his forest. When Hidimbi saw Bhima, the second Pandava, she was so overwhelmed by desire that she decided to protect rather than harm the Pandavas and their mother. She informed Bhima of her brother's intention and offered to take him and his family to safety. The mighty Bhima declined the offer, as he was quite capable of protecting his family on his own. Bhima attacked and killed Hidimba. Instead of mourning for her brother, Hidimbi followed the Pandavas and begged their mother Kunti for Bhima's hand in marriage. Kunti accepted her as daughter-in-law on condition that she enjoy his company only during the day and that she let him go after he had given her a child. Every daybreak, over the following weeks, Hidimbi would carry Bhima to a picturesque mist-covered hill where they would make love until nightfall. In time she bore Bhima a son called

Ghatotkacha. As soon as he was born, she bid her lover farewell and returned to the forest.

Mahabharata

Nowadays the self-choice ceremony does not exist. Indeed, love marriages are disapproved of in most orthodox Hindu families because love does not take language, caste, or social and economic status into consideration. Self-choice ceremonies and free love are still practiced among some tribes in central India. The woman shows her approval by accepting a gift of *pan* from the man.

Pan is a packet of betel leaf containing betel nuts and other aromatic fillings. It is chewed after meals to help digestion. It makes the mouth fragrant and the lips red. It is a symbol of luxury and an important ingredient in love play. Some say that when made by the lover, pan comes to possess aphrodisiacal properties. Even today a beautiful woman is not supposed to offer pan to or accept it from anyone except her husband.

Quest for a Wife

In ancient India, when a woman chose a man as her husband he was bound by propriety to marry her:

One day, as Krishna was taking a walk in the woods, he was approached by the river-nymph Kalindi, daughter of the sun-god Surya. "I have been traveling the world looking for my lord. I have finally found him in you. Please accept me as your wife." Krishna took Kalindi to the city of Dwarka

and married her according to rites laid down in the scriptures.

Bhagvata Purana

To be chosen by a woman of her own free will was a great honor for a man. However, unchosen men also sought to repay their debts to ancestors and gain access to worldly wealth. These men could either buy a wife or carry her off by force. Buying a wife was considered the way of asuras, or demons:

The sage Ruchika wanted to marry Satyavati. "Only if you give me a thousand white horses with black ears," said her father, Gadhi. Ruchika used his magic powers to fulfill the condition and married the woman he desired.

Mahabharata

Abducting a wife was considered the way of barbarians, or rakshasas. Warriors and kings commonly adopted this method of marriage, which they found an effective way of making political alliances:

Arjuna, the third Pandava prince, once paid a visit to the city of Dwarka, where he saw the beautiful princess Subhadra. Overwhelmed by desire, he rushed through the crowded streets on his chariot, seized the beautiful girl, and carried her off. Balarama, Subhadra's brother who wanted her to marry the Kaurava prince Duryodhana, was so angry when he learned of the abduction that he decided to pursue Arjuna and cut off his hands. But he was stopped by Subhadra's other brother, Krishna, who pointed out that

it was indeed an honor to have as brother-in-law a man who was brave enough to risk death in his quest to marry the woman he loved.

Mahabharata

In some versions of this story Krishna, who had advised Arjuna to abduct the woman he loved, also told Subhadra to hold the reins of the chariot as they rode out of the city to inform the Yadavas that she was leaving of her own free will.

The most approved form of marriage, however, was the way of Prajapati, lord of progeny: For the sake of procreation, a father selflessly gave his daughter to any man who wanted to have children by her. There was no transaction.

Protecting the Wife

After obtaining a wife, the husband was terrified of losing her. In one moving love story the husband prefers to give up half his life rather than lose his wife to the god of death. This story stands out in sacred Hindu lore as one of the few stories in which a the man finds life without his wife worse than death:

On the day of her wedding Pramadvara died of a snakebite. The heartbroken groom, Ruru, invoked the gods and threatened to kill himself if she was not brought to life. So the gods consulted Yama, god of death, and agreed to let Pramadvara live, if Ruru gave half his life to her. Ruru accepted this arrangement and Pramadvara came back to life.

Devi Bhagvatam

Because wives were so precious, husbands fought hard to protect them from philanderers:

Utathya married Bhadra, a woman of extraordinary beauty. Varuna, the sea-god, saw her and, overcome by desire, abducted her from the sage's hermitage. In holy rage, Utathya drank up all the rivers, lakes, seas, and oceans until there was not a drop of moisture in the whole world. Only after Varuna had restored Bhadra did Utathya give back the waters to the parched earth.

Mahabharata

One sage was willing to shoot down the sun for daring to hurt his wife's delicate skin:

The sage Jamadagni was an archer. Every time he shot an arrow, his dutiful wife Renuka ran to pick it up. She would bring it back before Jamadagni could shoot the next arrow. One day she ran after an arrow and did not return until evening. On inquiry, she revealed that the harsh sun had blinded her and burnt her skin. So she had taken shelter under a tree until the sun set and the ground was cool. To teach the sun a lesson, the sage raised his bow and threatened to shoot down the sun-god Surya as he rode across the sky in his golden chariot. Surya begged for mercy and offered the sage's wife a pair of sandals and a parasol to protect her body from the harsh glares of the sun.

Mahabharata

The epic Ramayana tells the tale of how Rama punished Indra for daring to solicit his wife:

While wandering through the forest, Indra, king of the devas, cast his lustful eyes upon Sita. He took the form of a crow and tried to touch her. Sita took objection to this and complained to Rama. Rama picked up a blade of grass and with a magic formula converted it into a missile that he directed toward the crow. It punctured the crow's lustful eye. So it is that a crow has only one eye.

Ramayana, Agni Purana,
Padma Purana

When Ravana abducted Sita, Rama roused the forces of Nature to her rescue:

✳

During his fourteen-year exile, Rama's wife Sita was abducted by Ravana, the rakshasa-king. To rescue her, Rama roused the forces of Nature. Vultures flew into the sky and located Sita in the island kingdom of Lanka. Rama then raised an army of monkeys and bears, built a bridge across the sea that was held aloft by fishes and other sea creatures, and stormed Ravana's citadel. Because he had no horse or elephant to ride into battle, he rode on the shoulders of the monkey-god Hanuman and shot dead all the rakshasas, including Ravana, who stood between him and his beloved Sita.

Ramayana

The Ramayana has many folk versions. In southeastern Asian versions of the epic one learns of Rama's sorrow when he is tricked into believing that his beloved is dead:

✳

Ravana sent a sorceress to trick Rama into believing that Sita was dead. The sorceress appeared on the shores of the sea in the form of a rotting corpse. Rama recognized the ornaments on the dead body as those belonging to Sita. "Ravana must have killed her and thrown her body into the sea," he cried. As he lamented the loss of his beloved, Hanuman felt something was amiss. He ordered his monkeys to place the corpse on a pile of wood and lit the funeral pyre. As soon as fire engulfed the corpse, it jumped up and began to run toward the sea. Hanuman caught hold of the "dead body" and forced the sorceress to reveal all to Rama or risk a painful punishment.

Ramakien

In the epic Mahabharata the man who casts his lustful eyes on the common wife of the Pandavas pays with his life:

For a year the five Pandavas and their common wife Draupadi had to live incognito in the court of King Virata. Draupadi served as the queen's handmaiden and caught the attention of the queen's brother Kichaka, who ordered her to come to his chamber at night. Not knowing what to do, Draupadi sought the protection of her second husband, Bhima, the strongest of the Pandavas, who was working in the palace kitchens. Disguised as Draupadi, Bhima lay in Kichaka's bed. When Kichaka came to bed, Bhima crushed him to death as he tried to make love. In the morning, when Kichaka's mutilated body was discovered, Kichaka's brothers accused Draupadi of sorcery and tried to burn

her alive. Bhima entered the crematorium, uprooted a tree, and killed them all. With no witnesses to the murder, Bhima's identity as the king's cook remained secret.

Mahabharata

A Wife on Either Side

The wife reflects a husband's personality, strength, virility, and wealth. If she is ugly, unhappy, unsafe, unchaste, and poorly adorned, the husband is seen in a poor light. If she is beautiful, joyful, safe, chaste, and richly adorned, his prestige soars. If he has two such wives, he is considered a hero. If he has three, he is greater still. The number of happy women in the harem determined the worldly power and sexual prowess of gods, kings, and demons:

When the monkey-god Hanuman entered the island kingdom of Lanka in search of Rama's wife Sita who had been abducted by the rakshasa-king Ravana, he discovered on Ravana's bed several beautiful women writhing in sexual ecstasy. They were daughters of kings, sages, gandharvas, rakshasas, and asuras, who came there of their own accord, sometimes abandoning husbands, enamored by Ravana's beauty, splendor, and sexual prowess. Struck by arrows of the love-god, some women caressed and kissed other women who had been caressed and kissed by Ravana, in the hope of tasting the remains of the rakshasa-king's virility. Hanuman did not find Sita

A god with two consorts. Twentieth century calendar art.

among them. For she was devoted to Rama and in her chastity refused to even look upon the mighty lord of Lanka.

Ramayana

Many wives did not take kindly to a husband's second marriage:

Brahma decided to perform a yagna. While his consort Savitri went for a bath, he collected the necessary implements and utensils required to set up the altar. When all was done, there was no sign of Savitri. Brahma grew impatient. Because a yagna cannot be conducted without a wife, Brahma created another woman called Gayatri, married her, placed her next to him, and began the ceremony. When Savitri returned and discovered another woman sitting next to Brahma, she lost her temper. She cursed Brahma that he would not be worshipped in any temple.

Padma Purana

Co-wives often fought over the husband:

When the river-goddess Ganga descended from the heavens, the gods requested Shiva to break her fall lest she wash away the earth with the force of her waters. Shiva let her flow through his hair. Entangled in his mighty locks, Ganga's fierce torrent was transformed into a gentle stream, much to the satisfaction of the gods. However, Parvati, Shiva's consort, was not very happy to find Ganga sitting on Shiva's head. She demanded an explanation. "How is it that I, your lawfully wedded wife, sit on your lap
but you keep another woman on your head?" Ganga giggled, "If he lets me go, he knows I will wash away the world and he will be blamed for it." Realizing Shiva's predicament but unwilling to share her husband with the capricious river-goddess, Parvati fused her body with Shiva, becoming his left half, turning Ganga into an outsider, a concubine.

Folklore from northern India

In Shiva temples the base of Shiva's linga is formed by *bhaga*, the generative organ of Parvati. The two are eternally locked. Right above the linga hangs a conical pot that represents Ganga. Through a hole at the bottom of the pot, she keeps dripping water on the divine couple, making her presence felt.

Keeping two wives happy under one roof requires all the skill of Vishnu, the sustainer, renowned in the three worlds for his guile:

Vishnu's two wives, the goddess of sovereignty Shri and the goddess of earth Bhu, constantly sought his attention. Shri demanded it in her position as senior wife, Bhu secured it by using her submissiveness to make Vishnu feel guilty. Once Indra gave Vishnu the parijata tree. Both goddesses wanted it to be planted in their respective gardens, which were separated by a high wall. Vishnu gave the plant to Bhu, because she was the earth-goddess. Bhu immediately began flaunting her fertility and taunting Shri. To teach Bhu a lesson, Vishnu decreed that flowers would bloom only on the side of the tree facing Shri's garden. Shri would enjoy the fruits of Bhu's labor. Learning this, Shri began taunting Bhu. To teach Shri a lesson, Vishnu announced that the tree would only bloom when he would visit Bhu's

A man with three women—an expression of virility.
Twentieth century reproduction of medieval North Indian miniature.

garden. Thus every time Shri saw the flowers of parijata, she had to endure the knowledge that her lord was with someone else.

Folklore from southern India

Bhu and Shri are considered earthly and heavenly manifestations of Laxmi, goddess of wealth and fortune. When Vishnu descended upon the earth in the form of Krishna, they joined him as Rukmini and Satyabhama and the quarrels continued.

Plight of the Lonely Man

Some men did not even have one wife, let alone two. They had neither the charm to win a girl's heart nor the accomplishments to impress her father, neither the power to abduct a woman nor the wealth to buy one. In desperation these men took drastic measures:

Sumedhas and Somavat were two poor priests, or brahmanas. They sought wealth that would enable them to buy a wife. They were directed to the generous queen Simantini, who served lunch and offered rich gifts to one brahmana couple each day. The two youths were in a fix—they needed the gifts to get married but they could not get the gifts unless they were married. So they decided to obtain the gifts by deceit. Somavat disguised himself as a woman, and with Sumedhas acting as the "husband," they introduced themselves to the queen as a

brahmana "couple." Simantini welcomed them and treated them as manifestations of Shiva and Shakti. Such was the power of her piety that Somavat lost his manliness and became a woman. Sumedhas married his former friend. With the gifts they received, the two set up a house where they lived happily ever after.

Skanda Purana

While the preceding story has homoerotic undercurrents, the following story tells the story of a man who, in his quest to know the love of a wife, ends up becoming the patron god of eunuchs and transvestites:

During the battle at Kurukshetra, the Pandavas were informed by oracles that they would not win unless a youth with a flawless body was sacrificed to the goddess Kali, mistress of battlefields. Arjuna's son by the naga princess Ulupi, Aravan, matched the requirements perfectly. The young man agreed to be sacrificed for the sake of his family on one condition—that he be given a wife for one night. The Pandavas looked around for a wife, but no one was willing to marry a man doomed to die the very next day. Finally, Krishna, friend of the Pandavas, came up with a solution. He transformed himself into a ravishing woman called Mohini, married Aravan, spent the night with him, and, at dawn, after Aravan was sacrificed, mourned his death like a widow, beating his breast and unbinding his hair. In death Aravan became Khoothandavar, the deity who marries eunuchs and transvestites for a night before his annual death.

Khoothandavar Sthala Purana,
from the state of Tamil Nadu

Brothers could fall apart on the issue of marriage:

Prajapati Vishvarupa wanted his daughter to marry either Kartikeya or Ganesha, the two sons of Shiva. Shiva declared that the first of his sons to go around the world thrice would marry the girl. Kartikeya immediately mounted a peacock and started his journey. Ganesha mounted a mouse and simply went around his parents three times. "My parents are my world," he said and claimed the prize. Shiva was so pleased with Ganesha's wit that he let him marry Prajapati Vishvarupa's daughter. Kartikeya, who had actually gone around the world three times, felt cheated. In his fury he left his father's abode in the icy northern hills and sought refuge in the hot southern forests.

Folklore from northern India

A Victim of Rape

There was one scripturally recognized but universally disapproved-of option that the lonely man could turn to in order to win a wife—rape!

Although ideally, a woman had to be invited to bed, marriage by rape has also been documented in sacred Hindu lore. This form of marriage—by impregnating a woman while she is drunk or sleeping—was considered the way of vampires, or pisachas:

The warrior woman Ali refused to marry the Pandava Arjuna. Once he entered her bedroom in the form of a swan and crooned his

love to her, but she shooed him away. She even threatened to kill him. Finally, Arjuna sought the help of his mentor Krishna, who suggested that he marry her in her sleep. Taking the form of a serpent, Arjuna slipped into Ali's bed and made love to her as she slept. Krishna solemnized the union.

Folklore from the
state of Tamil Nadu

The ancients realized that while a man needed to be aroused for his seed to flow, a woman's will was not vital to produce a child. However, the mother-goddess did not appreciate any man, even her own son, coercing a woman to have sex:

Kartikeya, son of Shiva and Parvati, was commander of the celestial forces. After killing the asura Taraka, he was so full of passion that he wanted to make love to every woman who crossed his path. The women went to Parvati and informed her of Kartikeya's unwarranted sexual attentions. The goddess decided to teach Kartikeya a lesson—every time he tried to force himself on a woman, he discovered that she looked just like his mother. Realizing that all women were aspects of Parvati, he swore never to marry a woman unless she came to him willingly.

Brahmanda Purana

Although nymphs were considered free spirits of Nature, forcing them to have sex was not acceptable:

While riding through the forest, Ravana saw Rambha, the celestial courtesan, and desired

to have sex with her. "I love your nephew Nalakubera and look upon you as my father-in-law," she said. But Ravana, overwhelmed by lust, ignored her protests and had his way with her. When Nalakubera learned of this, he cursed Ravana: "If Ravana ever forces a woman to have sex against her will, his head will burst into a thousand pieces."

Ramayana

Some women preferred death to dishonor. One woman killed herself and swore to be reborn as her rapist's nemesis:

Vedavati was performing austerities when Ravana, lord of the rakshasas, came into her hermitage and tried to rape her. To save herself, Vedavati jumped into the fire altar and burnt herself to death. Nine months later Ravana's wife Mandodari gave birth to a girl-child. Oracles discovered that she was Vedavati reborn. "Kill the child who will kill you," they said. So Ravana threw the child into the sea. The sea-god saved it and gave it to the earth-goddess, who gave her to Janaka, king of Mithila. The child was named Sita, "she who was furrowed out of the earth." She went on to be the cause of Ravana's death.

Ramayana, Devi Bhagvatam

Wives who were forced to have sex against their will could reject husbands:

Dirghatamas followed the path of animals and believed in free sex. He tried to have sex with his sister-in-law, but she threw him out. He

*forced his wife Pradveshi to prostitute herself
so that he could live off her earnings. Disgusted
by his ways, Pradveshi and her son Gautama
threw him into a river. He would surely have
died had he not clung to a floating tree.*

Mahabharata

When a king turned rapist, not only he but
his entire kingdom was penalized, for as king
he formed the moral foundation of his realm:

*King Danda ruled a prosperous kingdom that
stood between the northern plains and the
southern plateau of India. One day, while
out on a hunt, he came upon the beautiful
Ara, all alone in her father's hermitage.
Overwhelmed by lust, Danda caught hold
of her, pinned her to the ground, and forced
himself on her. To avenge her dishonor, Ara
performed austerities until Indra, king of
devas and lord of fertility, let it rain fire upon
Danda's kingdom.*

Ramayana

After Indra had destroyed Danda's kingdom, it turned into the dense forest of
Dandaka, where even birds and beasts feared
to tread.

Death in the Womb

Nature does not recognize rape. Ancestors are
not fickle about the womb they are conceived
in. So long as a seed is shed in a fertile womb,
a child is conceived. Whether the seed belongs
to husband, lover, rapist, or brother does not
matter:

*After her monthly period, Yagnavalkya's
widowed sister Kamsari covered her genitals with a piece of cloth that, unknown to
her, was stained with her brother's semen.
When she became pregnant she was filled
with shame. Not knowing the cause of pregnancy, she abandoned the child under a pi-
pal tree, hence the child came to be known
as Pippalada. Yagnavalkya divined what had
occurred and consoled his sister, saying it
was no fault of hers.*

Skanda Purana

The gods, determined to rotate the cycle
of life, do not grant a woman the power to
reject an unwanted seed. Whether she was
seduced or raped, her womb accepted semen
and conceived a child. All a victim of rape
can do is try to abort the fetus:

*Ugrasena of the Yadava clan ruled Mathura.
His wife Padmavati was raped by the demon Gobhila. When she discovered she was
pregnant, she tried to abort the fetus, but all
her attempts failed. In despair she went
through with the pregnancy and delivered the
fruit of her rapist's seed. She cursed the re-
silient newborn named Kamsa that he would
die at the hands of her husband's kinsman.*

Padma Purana

A woman may want to reject an unwanted
fetus, but the gods do not support her desire.
She could even end up paying a heavier price
than the rapist:

Mamata, the wife of Utathya, was pregnant when her brother-in-law Brihaspati raped her. Mamata rejected Brihaspati's seed, preferring to keep in her womb her husband's child. Brihaspati also refused to take responsibility for the rejected seed. The gods nurtured the abandoned seed while condemning the child in Mamata's womb to be born blind.

Mahabharata

Attempting to kill an unborn child is considered a greater sin than rape. The former goes against the cycle of life. The latter, though reprehensible, supports the cycle of life. A man who tries to abort a fetus is struck with a curse:

The monkey-king Vali was threatened by the news that the chaste Anjani, wife of the Kesari, was pregnant with Hanuman, a divine monkey blessed with the strength of thunder. To secure his throne, he made a missile with five metals and shot it into Anjani's womb. On contact with the fetus inside, the missile melted and turned into earrings for Hanuman. For attempting to harm a defenseless fetus, Vali was cursed with helplessness at the time of his death. Vali was shot dead by an arrow shot deceitfully from the back while he was busy trying to fend off a pretender to his throne.

Kamban Ramayana, folklore
from the state of Orissa

Even Indra, king of the gods, performs austerities to wash away the sin of abortion:

When Indra learned that Diti was pregnant with a child who would grow up to be more powerful than him, he released a thunderbolt and cut the unborn child into forty-nine pieces. The cries of the unborn child could be heard across the cosmos. They became the forty-nine howling storm-gods. For this heinous crime, Indra lost his celestial crown. He had to perform penance for a thousand years to wash away the sin of abortion. The storm-gods were adopted by Shiva, and they were ultimately accepted as Indra's companions.

Rig Veda, Vishnu Purana

In the epic Mahabharata the character Ashvathama is cursed to suffer for eternity for the sin of trying to cause miscarriage:

The Pandavas defeated the Kauravas in battle. Unwilling to accept defeat, one of the Kaurava warlords named Ashvathama decided to kill all Pandavas by deceit. He entered their encampment in the middle of the night and slaughtered five warriors whom he thought were the five Pandavas. They turned out to be the five sons of the Pandavas by Draupadi. Draupadi, inconsolable on learning of the murder, demanded that Ashvathama be killed. In a bid to escape, Ashvatama shot an arrow into Uttara's womb. Uttara was the daughter-in-law of the Pandavas. In her womb was the last of the Pandava heirs. The unborn child would surely have died had Krishna not used his magic powers to stop the arrow. For trying to harm a fetus, Krishna cursed Ashvathama that his battle wounds would never heal. No herb would allay his

A mother with her child.
Stone carving from the queen's
stepwell of Patan, Gujarat.
Eleventh century.

*suffering, and even death would not come
to ease his pain.*

Mahabharata

Ashvathama's suffering is a Hindu metaphor for never-ending agony—the fate of a man who tries to halt the cycle of life.

Killing Women

Killing a woman was considered as great a sin as abortion because it was tantamount to killing all the children she would bear. In ancient India the code of warriors prevented men from raising weapons against women:

In the battle at Kurukshetra the Pandavas found it impossible to defeat Bhisma, commander of the Kaurava army. So they decided to use guile. It was known that Bhisma could not be defeated as long as he held weapons. It was also known that he would not raise his weapons against a woman. So Arjuna the warrior rode into battle with Shikhandi as his human shield. Shikhandi was born a woman but had acquired the body of a man later in life through the magical grace of yakshas. When Bhisma saw Shikhandi, he lowered his weapons, refusing to fight one who was, at core, a woman. Taking advantage of this situation, Arjuna shot Bhisma down with a rain of arrows.

Mahabharata

Even Vishnu, guardian of the cosmos, cannot escape the consequences of killing a woman:

Once while their guru Kavya was away, the asuras took shelter in the house of Kavya's mother, Pulomi. When their eternal enemies, the devas, launched an attack on Pulomi's house, Pulomi decided to use a magic formula to put the gods to sleep. But just as she was about to chant the mantra, Vishnu flung his sharp-edged discus and cut her throat. For killing a woman, Vishnu was struck with a curse that he would be born on earth seven times over and each time experience the same fear of death as any mortal.

Matsya Purana

Survival of a people has always depended more on the number of women than that of men. If a tribe of ten men and ten women is struck by an epidemic, the chances of the tribe repopulating itself is greater if the epidemic kills nine men than if it kills nine women. Perhaps that is why women were forbidden from bearing arms and participating in battle. If women survive, the clan survives. The womb contains the nectar of immortality for a race:

The warrior caste of kshatriyas was given military might by the gods to protect the earth. Corrupted by power, warriors used their weapons to dominate society. Once they raided the hermitage of sage Jamadagni to steal his cows. When Jamadagni tried to stop them, they killed him. At the sage's funeral, his son Parashurama watched his widowed mother, Renuka, beat her chest twenty-one times in sorrow. In his rage he picked up an ax and swore to attack the kshatriyas twenty-one times and wipe out the warrior caste from the face of the earth.

Parashurama succeeded in his mission and ended up filling ten lakes with kshatriya blood. Knowing that Parashurama would never harm women, one warrior named Valika saved himself by hiding in the female quarters of his father's palace. He became renowned as Nari-kavacha, "he whose armor is made up of women." He went on to impregnate all the kshatriya widows and repopulate his caste. Thus future generations of warriors sprang out of a single man.

Mahabharata

Harming a woman is seen as harming the nourisher of life, hence sinful. By the same logic, harming the earth is considered a sin in Hinduism. In sacred Hindu lore the earth is depicted as a divine cow whose milk nourishes plants and animals:

Once the earth-goddess Bhudevi, angered by the ingratitude of all beings, refused to let seeds germinate and trees bear fruit. The resulting famine caused havoc on earth. Moved by the lamentations of starving children, Vishnu took the form of the universal sovereign Prithu and threatened Bhudevi with dire consequences if she did not feed his subjects. Undaunted by the threat, the earth-goddess took the form of a cow and ran away. Prithu mounted his chariot and pursued the earth-cow. When he finally managed to corner her, he raised his bow and threatened to shoot her down. "If you kill me, I will die and so will all your subjects, because only I can nourish them," said the earth-cow. Prithu lowered his bow and reasoned with the earth-cow. She finally consented on the condition that Prithu protect her from abuse. Prithu swore that his subjects would never abuse the

earth, and should they do otherwise, they would face the wrath of Vishnu. Thus Vishnu became the guardian of the earth-cow. When ambition broke the earth-cow's back and greed hurt her teats, the earth-cow complained to her guardian Vishnu, who descended upon the earth and annihilated the ambitious and greedy people of the world.

Bhagvata Purana

Prithu institutes the practice of prudent economics and teaches man how to milk the earth's resources without harming her. He exhorts all to love and protect the earth-cow. If she is taken care of she can provide milk for food and dung for fuel for all eternity. Plundering her resources is akin to cutting her flesh and drinking her blood, which would benefit no one in the long run. To drive home this point, sacred Hindu law recommends the worship of cows and forbids the eating of beef. It is interesting to note that sacred Hindu lore has always considered the earth a living organism, long before the Gaia hypothesis was propounded by scientists and ecologists of the twentieth century.

Union of Man and Woman

In the Hindu marriage ceremony a man and woman become husband and wife after they take seven steps together in the presence of relatives and the sacred fire. Each step represents one of the seven worldly things that bind them together—food, strength, wealth, pleasure, progeny, cattle, and friendship. As the ends of their garments are tied together, the groom takes the hand of the bride with the words, "I seize your hand that I may gain fortune; I am the spirit, you are the rest; I am the words, you are the melody; I am the seed, you are the field; I am the sky, you are the earth."

Ancient Hindu priests converted the sexual union of man and woman into a ritual known as the sacrament of conception, or *garbhadhana samskara*. This union is sacred because it creates a portal between the land of the dead and the land of the living, enabling ancestors to reenter samsara. The act unites spirit with matter. Sex helps the wheel of life go around.

This now-obsolete ritual began with an invitation to the wife during her fertile period: "Being happy in mind, here mount the bed; give birth to children for me, your husband." Before penetrating her, he touched her vulva and recited sacred verses. "Let Vishnu prepare your womb; let Tvastr adorn your form; let Prajapati pour on; let Dhatar place the embryo. Hold the embryo, O Sarasvati; let both the Ashwini garlanded with blue lotuses set it in place." After shedding his semen, reclining over her right shoulder, he placed his hand between her breasts and said, "You whose hair is well parted—I know your heart that dwells in the moon. May it know me, too. May we see a hundred autumns together."

So sacred is the sexual act that its interruption leads to dire consequences:

To enjoy sex in the open, without any inhibitions, the sage Kindama and his wife took the form of a buck and a doe. While he was mounting her, Pandu, lord of the Kuru clan, accidentally shot an arrow that pierced both their hearts. Just before he died, Kindama cursed Pandu: "You will die if ever you touch a woman amorously." Pandu realized the implications of the curse—he would never be able to father

a child. In despair, he gave up his kingdom and decided to live like a hermit in the forest.

Mahabharata

According to the following little-known tale, even the sea is salty to remind children never to interrupt parents when they are making love:

Viraja had borne Krishna seven sons. Once she sought his company in the seclusion of a forest. At the height of their lovemaking, her youngest son interrupted them and complained that his elder brothers were troubling him. Krishna let go of Viraja, lovingly picked up the child, placed him on his lap, and wiped his tears. Angered by this unwarranted interruption of her pleasure, Viraja cursed her son to turn into the sea whose salty waters can never quench thirst.

Brahmavaivarta Purana

Images of man and woman in passionate embrace are a mandatory part of every Hindu temple because they affirm worldly life. Vaishnavas, worshippers of Vishnu, say that the cycle of life rotates forever because Vishnu in the form of Krishna is eternally sporting with his consort Radha in his celestial garden. According to the Shaivas, worshippers of Shiva, the cosmos exists only because Shiva and his consort Shakti are making love. Shaktas, worshippers of the mother-goddess, warn all creatures not to interrupt the goddess while she is sporting with her lord:

Once, when the goddess was sporting with Shiva, a group of sages entered their cave.

Image of man and woman in amorous embrace on a temple wall, symbolizing interdependence and wholeness. Stone carving; Khajuraho temple. Twelfth century.

Embarrassed, the goddess covered her nakedness. To please her, Shiva took her to a grove and decreed that any male who entered her sacred grove would turn into a woman. Unaware of this decree, Ila rode into the grove on a horse and discovered that he had acquired the body of a woman while his horse had turned into a mare.

Bhavishya Purana

In popular belief only the celestial beings known as devas are childless. In some stories this is because, having consumed the nectar of immortality, they have no need for offspring. In other stories, however, the devas were cursed to remain childless because they interrupted the lovemaking of the goddess.

Love Charms of a Woman

A woman's role in sex is seen as that of the recipient. She is looked upon as the altar of a Vedic yagna, passively waiting for the priest to offer oblation. In the Brihadaranyaka Upanishad one is told, "Woman is fire—the phallus is her fuel; the hairs are her smoke; her vulva is her flame; when man penetrates her, that is her coal; her ecstasy is her sparks. In this very fire gods offer semen; from this oblation man comes into being." Yagnas were Vedic ceremonies that, like sex, maintained the integrity of the cycle of life. During yagnas, priests made offerings to empower gods in their battles against the demons. But the gods could receive the oblations only if the offering was made in a fire burning on specially designed altars. In sex woman is the altar, man is the priest. Unless the altar prepares herself to receive the offering, the yagna of sex reaps no rewards. The womb has to be ripe and the body, beautiful.

The Hindu law books known as Dharmashatras exhort Hindu women in their fertile period to adorn themselves with flowers, cosmetics, and jewels and make themselves as alluring as the bright and fragrant flowers that attract bees. Adornment, or *shringara*, is thus not a feminine whim, but a sacred duty. It makes a woman's body auspicious. Under no circumstances is she to leave her body unadorned:

The machinations of his stepmother, Kaikeyi, forced Rama, prince of Ayodhya, to leave his father's city and live in the forest like a hermit for fourteen years. Sita, his dutiful wife, was bound by the laws of marriage to share his misfortune and follow him to the forest. However, when she began removing her royal finery in order to wear clothes of bark, as befits the wife of a hermit, the royal women stopped her. "It is unbecoming for a married woman to remove the jewels that adorn her body," they said. "Even if circumstances have forced your husband to become a hermit, you must continue to wear flowers, jewelry, cosmetics, and bright clothes." When Sita followed her husband to the forest, she was given enough clothes and jewels to suffice her for the period of exile. While in the forest she met Anasuya, wife of sage Atri, who gave her similar advice. The wife of the sage also gave her magical apparel that was never tainted on use.

Ramayana

Hindu women wear sixteen love charms, or *solah-shringara*, to arouse their husbands—earring, nose ring, toe ring, finger ring, bracelet,

A princess beautifying herself in her toilet. Mural at Mattencheri palace, Kerala. Seventeenth century.

armlet, anklet, waistband, necklace, hairpins, flowers, perfumes, kohl, red sari, vermilion mark on the forehead, and fragrant nuts in the mouth that stain the lips red. These are symbols of a *suhagan,* an unwidowed matriarch. These were gifts of Soundarya-Laxmi, goddess of beauty:

No one wanted to marry Rati, daughter of Brahma, because she was ugly. So Rati invoked the goddess Laxmi, who personifies Nature's beauty. The goddess gave Rati sixteen love charms. "With these," said the goddess, "all women will look appealing to men." When Rati adorned herself with these love charms, she looked so beautiful that Kama, the god of love, fell in love with her and made her his consort.

Folklore from Orissa

Even a poor man's wife was expected to beautify herself with whatever resources she had on hand:

Parvati, the mountain-princess, had married Shiva, the mountain-hermit, of her own free will. She shared his ascetic lifestyle without complaint. One day, however, she saw a group of goddesses bedecked in jewels and became very conscious of her simple clothing. Shiva divined her unhappiness and caused the rudraksha tree to grow. "Use the seeds of this plant as beads and make ornaments that befits a hermit's bride," he said. This made Parvati very happy. To worshippers of Shiva, ornaments made of Rudraksha beads are more precious than gems.

Folklore from the state of Bengal

The best reward for a woman was beauty. As in the following story, she could use it to win the hearts of sages or marry powerful kings:

Matsya was a fisherman's foster daughter. She was sometimes referred to as Gandhavati, "smelly one," because constant association with fish had given her body a fishy odor. Gandhavati rowed travelers across the river in the hope that the good deed would win her a good husband. One day the sage Parasara requested her to take to the other bank. Midstream, he expressed his desire to have sex with her. Fearing a curse if she refused, Gandhavati gave in. The sage drew a curtain of mist and made love to the terrified fisherwoman on an island in the middle of a river. Such was the spiritual prowess of Parasara that a child was born instantly and Gandhavati's virginity was restored. The sage rewarded Gandhavati by transforming her fishy body odor into an erotic fragrance. It so aroused Shantanu, king of Hastinapur, that he agreed to make the fisherwoman his queen.

Mahabharata

A woman's beauty stirs male virility. Her adornment and his arousal are important in the rites of conception. If a woman was ugly, as Apala is in the following story, she appealed to the gods to help her fulfill her womanly duties:

Apala's husband refused to touch her because she had a skin disease. Distraught, Apala called upon the gods. But no one answered her prayers. Then one day she accidentally chewed a twig of the soma plant whose juice

is much loved by the devas. Instantly, Indra, the king of devas, appeared before her. He pulled her thrice through the hole of his chariot wheel and caused her skin to slough. The first time, the sloughed skin turned into a hedgehog. The second time it turned into an alligator. The third time it turned into a chameleon. Having shed her skin three times, Apala's skin became smooth and radiant. Indra then made love to her and restored her fertility. Pubic hairs emerged and her womb ripened.

Rig Veda

The following story narrated by tribal bards from central India captures the plight of an ugly woman while explaining the male obsession for chewing tobacco:

Tambaku was the daughter of a tribal chief. She was so ugly that no man wanted to marry her. Her father offered all his wealth to the man who agreed to accept Tambaku as bride. However, even the lure of wealth did not win Tambaku a husband. Tambaku died of loneliness. The gods who had given her an ugly face felt responsible for her unhappiness. To make amends, they declared that in her next birth all men would desire her. Tambaku was therefore reborn as the tobacco plant whose leaves never leave the mouths of virile men.

Tribal lore from Madhya Pradesh

A woman's arousal is not as important as male arousal in the rites of conception. In its absence a child can still be conceived. However, according to ancient medical treatises, female arousal ensures that the child conceived is a healthy one. An unhappy woman in bed gives birth only to unhealthy children:

Vichitravirya died before he could impregnate his two wives, Ambika and Ambalika. So his mother, Satyavati, called upon the sage Vyasa to shed his seed in the two women. Vyasa, whose body had grown emaciated after years of austerity, requested time to beautify his body before entering the bedchamber of these women. But Satyavati was impatient for a grandchild and she forced Vyasa to visit the women when they were next in their fertile period. When Vyasa visited Ambika, she shut her eyes in fear. As a result, she gave birth to a blind son called Dhritarashtra. When Vyasa visited Ambalika, she paled on seeing his gaunt features. As a result, she gave birth to a pale child who was named Pandu. When it was time to visit Ambika again, Vyasa discovered in bed her low-caste handmaiden, who made love without fear. She gave birth to a healthy child called Vidura.

Mahabharata

A woman, determined to have healthy and happy children, could refuse to make love to her husband unless he adorned himself before coming to her:

Lopamudra discarded all finery and, dressed in clothes of bark, performed austerities along with her husband, the sage Agastya. Then one day, desiring offspring, he decided to make love to her. "I will not approach you dressed in rags of asceticism. Bedeck me and yourself in silks and gold, then I shall come

to you." To fulfill his wife's wish, Agastya went around the world and, after various adventures, collected enough wealth to do as his wife desired. As promised, she approached him with love in her heart and desire in her loins.

Mahabharata

If quality was not important, male adornment and female arousal were not considered vital in the rite of conception.

Rights in the Fertile Period

A husband was obliged to make love to his wife whenever her womb was ripe to accept seed. The shedding of menstrual blood indicates death, the inability of a man and woman to come together at the right hour to help another ancestor's rebirth. Both the man and the woman responsible incurred the sin of abortion. The law books therefore describe a woman in her periods as a *chandali*, "one polluted by a corpse." She was expected to isolate herself as the womb shed blood. When the bleeding stopped, she was told to bathe, beautify herself, and present herself to a man.

If a husband could not satisfy the wife during her fertile period, he had to arrange for another man to do the needful. Such a relationship was not considered adulterous, because it enabled the rebirth of an ancestor:

The sage Veda once went on a pilgrimage, leaving his disciple Uttanka in charge of the hermitage. While he was away, Veda's wife menstruated. In the following fertile period she invited Uttanka to her bed. "Because my husband is away and my womb is ripe,

you should replace the master of the house,"
she explained. With great unease, Uttanka
did what was to be done. When Veda re-
turned, he heard what had transpired. He
told Uttanka that he had done the right thing
and blessed him.

Mahabharata

It was said that a woman in her fertile period, all alone in bed, attracts the amorous eye
of Indra, king of devas. Husbands, therefore,
avoided staying away from home after their
wives had had their ritual bath following menstruation:

The sage Devashrama had to go on a pilgrim-
age, leaving behind his beautiful wife Ruchi in
the hermitage. He left his disciple Vipula in
charge. Fearing that Indra might arouse Ruchi's
passions, Vipula used his magic powers to en-
ter Ruchi's body. From within, he restrained
her from responding to Indra's amorous ad-
vances. Later, Vipula was embarrassed by his
intimate contact with his guru's wife Ruchi.
Devashrama reassured him that he did no
wrong, for his intentions were honorable.

Mahabharata

As lord of fertility, Indra gives women the
right to approach any man when she is in her
fertile period. This was used by many women
to their advantage in ancient times:

While Arjuna was bathing in a river, he was
abducted by the naga princess Ulupi, who
demanded that he give her a child. Arjuna
refused. Then Ulupi reminded her of his duty
as a man to offer seed to any woman who

demanded it. Arjuna relented and spent time
with Ulupi until she gave birth to their son,
Aravan.

Mahabharata

Under no circumstances could a man
refuse a woman who demanded sex during her
fertile period:

Diti approached her husband, the sage
Kashyapa, at twilight while he was perform-
ing rituals to ward off malevolent spirits of
the night. When she demanded that he come
to her, he said, "I will because I have to.
But the children that will be conceived will
have a demonic disposition." So it came to
pass. Diti gave birth to daityas who became
eternal enemies of the adityas, keepers of life,
light, and order.

Bhagvata Purana

Some women used this power to conceive
powerful children:

Kaikesi, daughter of the rakshasa-king
Sumali, wanted to have a son by the sage
Vaishrava who had fathered the mighty
Kubera, lord of treasures, on a yaksha
woman. So when the monthly flow of blood
stopped and her womb ripened, she went to
his hermitage. The sage agreed to embrace
her. In time Kaikesi gave birth to Ravana,
who went on to lead the rakshasas in battles
against the gods.

Ramayana

A man who rejected the solicitations of a
woman had to pay a terrible price:

Urvashi, the celestial nymph, desired Arjuna. However, Arjuna refused to entertain her, saying, "By embracing you I will incur the sin of incest. For you were once the wife of my ancestor Pururava." "Earthly laws do not apply to divine creatures," said Urvashi, but Arjuna was not convinced. Enraged, Urvashi cursed Arjuna: "May you lose your manhood." Thus Arjuna became a eunuch. By the grace of Indra, king of the gods, who was also Arjuna's father, the curse manifested itself only for a year.

Mahabharata

Only the grace of a god could save a man from the crime of rejecting a woman who desired him:

Devala was a handsome and intelligent priest well versed in the scriptures. The apsara Rambha fell in love with him, but because Devala had taken the vow of celibacy, he refused to have sex with her. Piqued by the rejection, Rambha cursed him that his body would crook at eight places. Devala thus became known as Ashtavakra, "he whose body is bent at eight places." Years later Krishna visited his hermitage along with Radha. Radha was shocked by the ugliness. So Krishna touched Devala and straightened his body.

Brahmavaivarata Purana

In the Brahmavaivarta Purana, the nymph Mohini says, "A man who refuses to make love to a woman tortured by desire is a eunuch. Whether a man be a householder, an ascetic, or a lover, he must not spurn a woman who approaches him, or he will go to hell."

Sap of Life

When a woman does not shed menstrual fluid after union with her husband, it indicates that a new life had been conceived. Retained menstrual fluid was believed to have the magical ability to ensheath the spirit with a thinking mind and a feeling body. It was considered the most visual manifestation of rasa, or creative energy. The dark red color of menstrual fluid became the color of life and fertility. Married Hindu women paint a red dot on their foreheads, wrap their bodies with red saris, and line their feet with red dye. Vermilion powder is an essential ingredient in all Hindu ceremonies. It enhances fertility and attracts good luck.

Like women, earth is also a vessel of fertility capable of creating and nourishing life. The creative power of rasa flows through earth as it flows through women. This link gave rise to some curious customs in ancient India. During spring festivals, kings invited beautiful women to the royal gardens to sing, dance, and embrace trees. Their presence and touch, it was believed, enhanced the creative power of earth and catalyzed the flowering of trees. The women thus helped plants transform into nymphs and seduce birds and bees with color, fragrance, and nectar. Images of women holding trees and creepers have become powerful fertility symbols that adorn the walls and gates of most Hindu temples.

Many Hindus believe that, like a woman, the earth menstruates and bears children. In summer, in the eastern state of Orissa, just before the monsoons, women observe *rojo*, the ceremony of the earth's menstruation. For three days the earth's blood-stained surface is considered polluted. All virgins stay indoors and avoid placing their feet on the ground. No work is done. On the fourth day there is great joy. The earth, represented by a grind-

*A tree nymph,
symbolizing the fertility
of Nature. Wall carving;
Rajarani temple, Orissa.
Twelfth century.*

ing stone, is washed with water as rasa flows again. Farmers begin tilling their fields. The seed is sown and the monsoons awaited.

Indra causes the rain to fall to satisfy the earth-goddess, warm with desire. As the weeks pass the seeds in her womb germinate, and tender green shoots emerge from the soil as if pulled by the rays of the sun. When this happens, women in the western state of Maharashtra celebrate Gauri Puja, the festival of the mother. Images of the goddess are adorned with green saris and green bangles as farmers acknowledge the visual manifestation of earth's renewed fertility.

A similar acknowledgment of a woman's fertility occurs in the ceremony known as *simanta,* celebrated in the seventh month of her first pregnancy. Dressed in green, the color of maternity, or red, the color of fertility, the mother-to-be is congratulated by suhagans, a group of women who are considered auspicious because their husbands are alive, children are healthy, and households prosperous. These women personify Nature at her benevolent best. The suhagans ward off malevolent spirits that could harm the fetus and pray for the safe delivery of the new child. They also part the mother's hair and stain the parting with vermilion, in anticipation of the day when her vaginal lips will part and blood-stained fluids will gush out as the womb releases a new life.

That will be a happy day. As the woman experiences birth pangs, priests will go about the house loosening all the knots to facilitate the loosening of the child from the womb. They will chant verses from the Atharva Veda: "Let the woman rightly engender, let her joints go apart, let the gods unclose her, let the vulval lips part, let the fetus not adhere to flesh, fat, or marrow and slip out, and then let the viscid spotted afterbirth descend for the dog to eat." After the umbilical cord is cut and the baby is washed, it will be presented to the breasts of the mother with a prayer: "May oceans full of milk, full of the divine nectar, abide in your breasts to strengthen your child." And as the child is being nursed, prayers will be said that it may "suck long life, suck wealth, suck strength." For the child will be no ordinary child. It will be a dead ancestor reborn.

Womb Worship

The womb, the renewer of life, is worthy of worship. It is the pot of immortality, *amrita-kumbha,* that keeps every family tree alive. Through it, ancestors regain access to another womb—that of the mother-goddess, defined by space and time, in which exists the endless splendors of the material world. Poets describe this celestial womb that cradles samsara as the basket of inexhaustible bounty, *akshaya-patra.*

Hindus worship the womb in the form of a container—sometimes a wicker basket, usually a pot. In sacred Hindu lore one often comes across stories in which a pot serves as a surrogate womb:

The sage Bharadvaja was taking his bath when he saw the water-nymph Ghritachi walking along the riverbank. The wind blew off her upper garment; a thorny bush caught and tugged at her lower garment. Bharadvaja thus caught sight of her splendid body—her full breasts and round buttocks. His passion roused, he could not restrain the emission of his seed. The seed fell into a pot and turned into a child. This child came to be known as Drona, "pot born."

Mahabharata

Without a pot, water cannot be collected, food cannot be gathered. Without a pot, there is hunger and thirst. A pot also symbolizes the milk-rich breasts of the mother-goddess that nourish all life. In Hindu kitchens one gets to hear of Draupadi's magical pot, which is always full of food:

Draupadi, wife of the Pandavas and queen of Indraprastha, was renowned for her hospitality. Whenever a sage visited the palace, she made sure he was well fed. When the Pandavas lost their kingdom and were forced into exile along with their queen, they went to the forest and sought refuge in caves. During this period, many well-wishing sages paid them a visit. Draupadi was heartbroken at being unable to feed them as she used to in the past. She invoked the goddess Laxmi and sought her help. The mother-goddess gave Draupadi a pot that would always be full of food. With this magical pot, Draupadi was able to feed her guests. No one who visited the Pandava caves ever left with an empty stomach. Thus was Draupadi's fame as a generous hostess restored.

Mahabharata

In folk rituals an effigy of the all-containing, all-giving mother-goddess is made by attaching a metal head to the rim of a pot. Filled with water, topped with a coconut, and ringed with a coronet of mango leaves, a pot transforms into *purna-kalasha,* or the "brimming urn" that ushers in fertility and fortune. The purna-kalasha is a permanent feature of all Hindu festivities related to marriage and childbirth. The pot represents the container of all things material. It is a vessel of fertility, the earth and the womb, nurturing and nourishing life without discrimination. The mango leaves, associated with Kama, god of love and lust, represent the pleasure principle that is an essential ingredient in fertility. The coconut, a cash crop in the tropical world, symbolizes prosperity. It also symbolizes the ego that makes its possible for one to relish power. The water in the pot is Nature's rasa, without which there can be no life on earth.

When a man dies, an earthen pot containing water is smashed to indicate the liberation of the spirit from the flesh. After the body is cremated, Hindus collect the ash in another earthen pot and, at the end of all funerary rites, throw the ashes in a river. Just as ashes from a pot enter the stream, it is hoped that ancestors, after a brief stay in the land of the dead, return to samsara to suckle once more the wonders of existence.

CHAPTER THREE

Dancing Nymphs

TRANSCENDING THE CIRCLE

Slippery Damsels of Delight

Samsara is not just the realm of worldly delights. It is also the realm of worldly suffering. Pleasure comes at the risk of pain; prosperity with the threat of poverty; power with a feeling of insecurity. Kama titillates the senses; artha inflates the ego; both ultimately betray the mind.

Worldly delights are like apsaras, the enchanting nymphs who forever grace the beds of the gods. In the arms of man they lie only until human inadequacy or mortality ensures their flight:

Pururava fell in love with the divine damsel Urvashi. She agreed to be with him so long as he took care of her pet goats and never showed her his nakedness. In her arms, in the dark, Pururava discovered the pleasure reserved for gods and thought of himself as a deva. One

night the flower-gods, the gandharvas, seeking the return of Urvashi to the celestial realms, stole her goats while Pururava and Urvashi were making love. The goats cried out, and Urvashi demanded that Pururava keep his promise. Pururava rushed after the thieves without bothering to cover himself. As he chased the thieves into the palace courtyard, Indra, king of devas, flashed his thunderbolt across the dark sky. In that light Urvashi saw Pururava's nakedness. When Pururava returned with the goats, Urvashi bid him farewell. "Can't I come with you?" begged Pururava. Urvashi shook her head and rose to the land of the immortals. Used to Urvashi's embrace, Pururava found no pleasure in the arms of mortal queens and concubines. In his unhappiness he misruled his people until they rose in revolt and killed him.

Mahabharata

Both nymphs and material delights provide eternal joy to the devas but slip out of human reach like water through a clenched fist. Both are available to anyone with enough strength to claim them. Neither has a heart. Neither knows what it means to be faithful. Kings come and go, but the kingdom and the concubine bring regal splendor to whoever wears the crown—hence the folk belief, "There have been many Indras in Amravati, but only one Sachi."

Sachi is the goddess of sovereignty and is identified with Shri, the fickle goddess of fortune whose favors are sought by devas and asuras:

Indra once lost his regal aura to Virochana, the asura. Consequently, he was driven out of Amravati. To find out the reason for the loss,

Indra took the form of a poor priest, obtained employment in Virochana's palace, and began serving the asura-king with devotion. During the course of his service, he learned that Virochana's virtue had earned him the affection of Shri. Some time later, pleased with his service, Virochana offered Indra a gift. "I want your virtue," said Indra. Virochana gave it away thoughtlessly and consequently lost the affection of Shri to Indra. With his royal aura restored through guile, Indra returned to Amravati and reclaimed his position as lord of the celestial spheres.

Shatapatha Brahmana

Tired of fickle goddesses and mercurial nymphs, man seeks eternity, permanence, certainty. When he fails to find it on earth, he looks heavenward.

Cast Out of Heaven

In the Vedic version of Urvashi's story, Pururava performs a yagna that transforms him into a gandharva and enables him to live with Urvashi in Amravati forever. Amravati is the divine realm of eternal life and endless joy. Vedic seers believed that by the power of yagna man could override his inadequacy and mortality to become a god. However, when he displayed human weaknesses in heaven, he lost all merits earned and was cast down to face once more the vicissitudes of mortal life:

Indra had to perform penance to wash away the sin of killing a priest. While he was away, someone was needed to serve as king of Amravati. The devas selected the mortal king

Nahusha because he had earned the merit of performing nearly a thousand yagnas. As temporary ruler of the celestial realms, Nahusha rode Indra's elephant, wielded his thunderbolt, walked in his pleasure gardens, and drank his wine. He was, however, never invited to enjoy the company of Indra's queen, Sachi. Nahusha demanded that privilege. To teach him a lesson, Sachi sent him a message: "Come to my bed as Indra did, on a litter carried by the seven cosmic seers." Nahusha immediately ordered the revered sages to serve as litter carriers. The sages obeyed out of deference to royal authority. On the way, impatient to be in Sachi's arms, Nahusha kicked one of the sages on his head. "Hurry up," he cried. The sage Bhrigu, disgusted by this display of unbridled carnality, cursed Nahusha to return to earth in the form of a serpent. Thus the man who dared dream of lying in Sachi's arms was reduced to crawling on his belly for the rest of his life.

Bhagvata Purana

Transgressors of heavenly codes who were cast down tried their best to make their stay on earth as short as possible. They preferred death to the experience of fear and insecurity that comes with mortal existence:

Mahabhisha's exemplary life as king, punctuated with numerous yagnas, earned him a place in the celestial city of Amravati beside Indra, king of the devas. One day the river-nymph Ganga paid a visit to Indra's court. As she entered the hall, her upper garment slipped and her bosom lay bare. The devas, in deference to the water-goddess, lowered their eyes. Mahabhisha, however, stared unashamedly. Disapproving of this behavior, Indra cursed Mahabhisha that he would be reborn on earth as the king Shantanu, fall in love with Ganga, and pay the price for wanting her. Ganga was also ordered to go to earth and return only after she had made the king aware of the pain that awaits one who seeks earthly pleasures. As she was leaving, Ganga was stopped by the eight vasus, gods of the elements, who had also been cursed to be born on earth for trying to steal the milk of the heavenly cow Kamadhenu. "While on earth, please be our mother and kill us as soon as we are born so that we may return quickly to Indra's paradise," they begged. So it came to pass. Mahabhisha was reborn as Shantanu and became king of Hastinapur. He met the beautiful Ganga on the banks of a river and was immediately in love. "I will marry you only if you never question my actions," she said. Shantanu accepted the condition and brought Ganga to his palace as queen. Ganga's lovemaking overwhelmed Shantanu. But there was a price to pay. Every time Ganga bore him a son, she would drown the newborn in the river. Shantanu, though horrified, did not protest, because he was bound by his word and bewitched by his desire. Ganga succeeded in killing seven sons of Shantanu. When she was about the kill the eighth child, Shantanu stopped her. "Stop, wicked woman, what kind of a mother are you?" he cried. By speaking out, Shantanu broke the marriage pact. As Ganga prepared to leave, she handed over her eighth son, named Devavrata, to her husband with the words, "What have you achieved by saving his life—he will never take a wife and so will never have access to the pleasures of worldly life. He will die childless, incurring the wrath of your ancestors."

Mahabharata, Devi Purana

Passage through Wombs

The womb introduces the soul to a realm of impermanence and sorrow. Some who did not want to face the wiles of worldly life, like the vasus, died as soon as they left the womb. Others avoided leaving the womb:

The sage Vyasa married Vatika, daughter of sage Jabali. In time she conceived a child. While he was in the womb, he heard his father recite the scriptures and epics. He learned about life on earth, about the fleeting pleasures of samsara, and made the decision not to leave his mother's womb. Twelve years passed and the fetus showed no signs of emerging. So Vyasa sought the help of Krishna, king of Dwarka, who was Vishnu incarnate. Krishna spoke to the child at length and taught him the means to break free from the cycle of life. Thus enlightened, the child emerged. He became renowned as Suka, "parrot," because he could rattle out the scriptures like a parrot.

Skanda Purana

When birth was unavoidable, some beings tried bypassing the womb. The *a-yoni-ja*, or nonwomb-born, was believed to be less susceptible to the tyranny of space and time. He had a greater chance of being unruffled by the vagaries of mortal existence:

Vamadeva acquired great wisdom at the moment of his conception. He invoked the gods and demanded that he be offered an alternate route out of his mother's body. Alarmed at the request, Indra tried to per-

suade the child to leave his mother's womb in the usual manner. But the child was determined to have his way. At the time of birth, he took the form of a kite and gnawed his way through his mother's flesh to emerge from her left side.

Rig Veda

One girl-child refused to leave her mother's womb until her father had accumulated enough good merit to ensure a good life for her on earth:

Gandini, princess of Kashi, refused to leave her mother's womb though the date of delivery had long passed. When her father entreated her to come out, she said, "Only after you give a cow a day for three years to the poor priests of your kingdom will I enter your realm." After the king of Kashi fulfilled his daughter's request, she emerged as promised.

Linga Purana

Liberation from a Merry-Go-Round

Heavenly spirits knew that the world beyond the womb seduces mortal flesh with the promises of unending orgasms. The resulting search generates so much karma that the soul is forever trapped in the wheel of existence—forgotten by the mind:

Narada once asked Vishnu, "What is the true nature of samsara?" In response Vishnu asked Narada to fetch him some water from a nearby river to quench his thirst. While collecting the water, Narada slipped and fell into the river. When he came out, he had acquired the body of a woman. A passerby looked at him admiringly, and Narada became aware of his feminine charm. The passerby begged Narada to marry him. Narada accepted the proposal, became a wife, and gave birth to sixty children. Together they built a house and established a prosperous farm on the riverbank. Surrounded by a loving husband, happy children, and a prosperous household, Narada experienced great joy. Then one day, after torrential rains, the river broke its banks and washed the farm away. Narada's husband and children were drowned in the flood. When the waters receded, Narada collected the corpses of her loved ones and carried them to a riverside crematorium. As she was about to light the funeral pyre, she experienced an extraordinary hunger. She looked around for some food and found a mango on the highest branch of a tree. To get to it, she piled the dead bodies of her husband and children on top of each other and climbed the pyramid of corpses. As she reached for the fruit, she slipped and fell into the river. "Help me, help me," Narada cried. Instantly, Vishnu pulled Narada out of the water. Narada suddenly found himself in Vishnu's presence with his male body restored. "Where is the water I sent you for?" asked Vishnu. Narada looked at the empty pot in his hand and realized he had forgotten all about his mission.

Bhagvata Purana

Narada is a renowned sage in sacred Hindu lore. He is one of Brahma's mind-born sons, celibate since childhood and untouched by desire. In the above story he is for the first time exposed to the illusory nature of worldly transformations. The experience convinces him to stay out of the cycle of life. He refuses to marry, produce children, and experience emotions that trap him in a meaningless merry-go-round of endless rebirths, oscillating forever between joy and sorrow. But these very emotions are what caused the cosmic spirit to be embodied by material reality in the first place:

In the beginning there was only Brahma. He was Swayambhu, "self-created." Desiring company, the lonely god created Shatarupa, goddess of material reality. Discomforted by the lust in her father's eyes, Shatarupa ran away, taking the form of a cow. Brahma followed her in the form of a bull. She then turned into a mare. He kept up the chase as a horse. When she turned into a goose, he became a gander. When she turned into a doe, he became a buck. Every time she transformed herself, he became the corresponding male, determined to possess her. Despite all efforts, he did not succeed. As the fruitless pursuit continued, all animals, from the smallest insect to the largest mammal, came into being.

Brihadaranyaka Upanishad,
Shatapatha Brahmana

Shatarupa transforms spontaneously, for such is the nature of matter. With each passing moment, she turns into something else. Her metamorphosis enchants Brahma, and he seeks to possess her. But she is mercurial—a series of momentary images. Any attempt to freeze her flow is bound to fail. Brahma tries nevertheless. He becomes Shatarupa's complement, losing his identity in the process. Brahma's action and the resulting series of reactions set in motion the wheel of existence.

A nymph, celebrating the world, and a monk, rejecting the world, flanking the god Vishnu, sustainer of the wheel of existence. Stone carving from the queen's stepwell of Patan, Gujarat. Eleventh century.

He generates the primal karma that fetters the soul to the flesh. He becomes the creator of samsara, unworthy of worship.

Shiva opposes Brahma's actions. He tries to stop Brahma from entangling the blissful soul in the throbbing sensuality of the flesh. He seeks to break every fetter, destroy all karmas, and liberate the soul. He becomes the destroyer of samsara, worthy of adoration:

Shatarupa's beauty so inflamed Brahma's passion that he sprouted five heads—four facing the cardinal directions, one on top—to look upon her at all times. With his fifth head, he voiced his erotic desires. Disgusted, Shatarupa ran away. Brahma pursued her, shouting obscenities with his fifth head. The commotion disturbed Shiva's meditation. Enraged by what was happening, he transformed into Bhairava, "fearsome one," and wrenched out Brahma's fifth head with his sharp claws. The violence restrained Brahma. Brahma's cut head seared into Shiva's hand. To detach the head, to clear his heart of the rage, Shiva went to Kashi and began meditating.

Shiva Purana, Bhavishya Purana

While meditating, Shiva does not respond to the consequences of his action. He thus burns up his karma, gradually unraveling the knots that tie the soul to the flesh. Brahma, as creator, cannot let Shiva do this. He decides to thwart Shiva's asceticism with the allure of a woman:

Sati was the daughter of Daksha, lord of civilization. She melted Shiva's austere heart with her undemanding love and became his wife. Shiva, unused to the ways of the world, did not salute his father-in-law. This irritated Daksha, who decided to get back at Shiva by not inviting him to a grand yagna. When Sati learned of her father's plan to insult her husband, she was furious. Shiva asked her to calm down; he was beyond such pettiness. But Sati did not listen. In her rage, Sati transformed into Kali, frightening Shiva himself. With a horde of cackling goblins, she went to her father's palace, disrupted the ritual, and leapt to her death in the sacrificial fire, contaminating the sacred precinct with her blood so that the ceremony ground to a halt. Incensed by the news of Sati's death, Shiva, in the form of the bloodthirsty warrior Virabhardra, beheaded Daksha. Then, clinging to Sati's charred corpse, he danced in sorrow, threatening to destroy the world with his grief until Vishnu, the sustainer, hurled his discus and cut Sati's corpse into a thousand pieces. With Sati's corpse gone, Shiva recovered his senses, entered a cave, and began meditating, determined to regain control over his mind.

Mahabhagvata Purana,
Brihaddharma Purana

Daksha is considered both a son and a manifestation of Brahma. He provides a wife for Shiva. Sati, the goddess of samsara, wins Shiva's heart with her devotion and breaks it with her stubbornness. Her transformation from Sati into Kali, from the docile consort to the uncontrollable termagant, generates torrents of emotions. Shiva grows so attached to her that he refuses even to part with her corpse. This attachment makes him angry, violent, and unhappy. It clouds his judgment. When the corpse is destroyed, he is liberated from his attachment and becomes aware of his delusion by mortal flesh. He wants no more of it. So he shrinks into a cave, shuts his eyes, restrains his senses, controls his breath, and ultimately regains control over his mind. He becomes the lord of yoga.

The word *yoga* stems from the root *yuja*, which means "to harness" or "to yoke." Yoga aims to yoke the mind so that it is not bewitched by the transformations of samsara. Yoga is essentially a mental discipline that enables one to take the beauty and the brutality of worldly life in stride. Shiva's yoga is inspired by his consort's transformation. It turns into a tool by which he detaches himself from material reality.

Shiva refuses to be part of worldly life and expresses this by not distinguishing between what is sacred and what is profane. He wanders in crematoria and dances in the light of funeral pyres. He makes no attempt to make himself presentable—he smears his handsome face with ash, wraps his body with untanned elephant hide, mats his hair with birch juice, and lets serpents slither round his neck. He sits atop Mount Kailas, the central axis of the Hindu cosmos, the nave of the wheel of existence, and—thanks to the power of yoga—remains unmoved while the world transforms around him.

Rejecting the Woman

Terrified by the hypnotic power of samsara, one sage turned away from the object of his earthly affection:

Bilvamangala's wife went to visit her parents, who lived on the other side of the river.

Unable to stay apart even for a single night, he decided to visit her secretly before daybreak. He went to the riverbank but found no boat. So he jumped into the river and, clinging to a log of wood, reached the other side. As he was scaling the wall of his wife's house holding on to a creeper, neighbors mistook him for a thief and raised an alarm. The whole village rushed to catch the "thief." When they recognized Bilvamangala and realized why he was trying to enter his wife's house in the middle of the night, they all began laughing. Bilvamangala's wife was so humiliated by the incident that she refused to let her husband in. "If your desire for the spirit matched your desire for the flesh, you would have attained liberation by now," she said and shut the door in his face. Shamed by her words, Bilvamangala returned home. On the way he discovered that the "creeper" he held on to while trying to climb the wall was in fact a python, and the "log" he had clung to while crossing the river was in fact a corpse. Lust had blinded him. "I must open my eyes wider and discover the ultimate truth that is eternal, unchanging, and unconditional," said Bilvamangala. So he renounced all desires and became an ascetic.

Folklore from the state of Bengal

Bilvamangala's rejection of his wife is essentially the rejection of worldly life. A woman offers pleasure, with pleasure come children, and with children come household responsibilities, the burden of duties, the need for power and property. Power and property inflate the ego, delude the mind, until nothing matters but the gratification of urges that fetter one forever to the cycle of endless rebirths. Death does not remove the craving for pleasure and power, kama and artha—the cry of pitris from the land of the dead is essentially their undead urge to indulge the flesh once more. Or maybe it is an appeal of the forefathers to embody themselves once more so that they can work toward moksha and liberate themselves from the tyranny of the senses that shackles them to the wheel of existence.

The journey away from the merry-go-round of worldly life usually begins with the rejection of a woman after being confronted with the dark side of worldly life:

A marriage was arranged between Nemi, a Yadava youth, and Rajimati, a Yadava maiden. On his marriage day Nemi heard the cries of animals and birds being slaughtered for the wedding banquet. "Can there be a world where such cries are never heard?" he wondered. To find the answer, Nemi walked away from the wedding altar and became an ascetic.

Kalpa Sutra

After walking away from the wedding altar, Nemi found the kind of world he was looking for, a realm where there was no pain, no suffering, only peace and quietude. Before leaving for this special place, he pointed out the path of liberation to all, earning the title of Tirthankara, "pathfinder." He also came to be revered as the *jina*, "he who triumphed over samsara." The path of the jina is known as Jainism.

The image of a jina is usually that of a naked man with a flaccid penis seated on a mountain with a serene smile on his face, unflustered by the brutality of the world around him, unimpressed by the beauty. He is almost like Shiva meditating atop Mount Kailas.

The Jains share the Hindu belief in samsara. However, they do not believe that there is a divine being out there responsible for it all. The Jain cycle of life is an impersonal entity. Within it, man has the choice of remaining either fettered or free. Freedom comes with austerities—such as yoga—that involve restraining the senses and controlling the mind. Freedom involves the liberation of blissful soul from the painful grip of matter.

The Buddhists, like the Jains, believe in an impersonal samsara. However, they do not believe in souls. They believe there is nothing permanent in this world. To them, the elixir of immortality is merely a figment of the imagination born of a mind terrified of death. The story of the founder of Buddhism, like that of Bilvamangala and Nemi, involves the rejection of a woman:

Prince Siddhartha Gautama of the Sakya clan was raised in a beautiful palace surrounded by beautiful people and beautiful things. When he came of age, he was given a beautiful wife called Yashodhara who in time bore him a beautiful son. But one day he went out of the city and discovered that life was not all beautiful. Out there, there was old age, sickness, and death. The idea that one day everyone—including Yashodhara—would age, become ill, and die made Siddhartha very unhappy. "Is there a remedy for this suffering?" he wondered. To find the answer, he slipped out of the palace, leaving behind his wife and child, became an ascetic, and eventually attained enlightenment.

Buddhist lore

To Hindus, Jains, and Buddhists, the female form embodied desire for all things material. She was the fetter who could even bewitch the gods:

Image of a Jain Tirthankara. Marble statue. Twentieth century.

Vishnu once descended from his heavenly abode in the form of a boar to raise the earth-goddess from the bottom of the sea. As they rose toward the surface, the earth-goddess assumed the form of a female boar. They made love, and the earth-goddess brought forth three sons. Vishnu's sons played together and spread havoc wherever they went. Paternal love prevented Vishnu from restraining his sons. His passion for his wife grew greater and he showed no signs of returning to heaven. Finally, Shiva took the form of a bull and gored Vishnu's sons to death. He then attacked Vishnu and released the god from the body of the boar.

Shiva Purana

Mortal flesh binds Vishnu to his wife. His enchanted mind prevents him from letting go, until Shiva, the great ascetic, destroys the mind-body sheath and liberates the spirit within.

Allure of the Nymph

The quest for liberation has its share of obstacles. Samsara does not let go easily. Just before Siddhartha discovered the cause of suffering and became the Buddha, he had to triumph over the daughters of Mara, the demon of desire. These women were at times as beautiful as nymphs and at times as ugly as ogresses. Their transformations reflected the allure and terror of samsara. They sought to seduce or frighten Siddhartha into submission. They failed.

Hindus know the daughters of Mara as apsaras, water-nymphs, daughters of the primal mage Kashyapa. With their transformations they, too, can arouse extreme emotions that make man part of worldly life:

King Durjaya was making love to Urvashi, the celestial courtesan, when he remembered his wife. He left Urvashi, promising to return as soon as he had fulfilled his husbandly duties. On his way back Durjaya met a gandharva who had an exquisite garland around his neck. Durjaya fought the gandharva and grabbed the garland. When Durjaya finally came to Urvashi with the stolen garland around his neck, he found Urvashi distant. She did not respond to his amorous advances. When he persisted, she transformed into a dark and hairy hag and scared him away.

Kurma Purana

When a sage seeks liberation from worldly life, he has to overpower the nymph, the personification of worldly pleasures:

The rishi Dadhichi performed austerities, bridling his senses and controlling his mind. The power of the asceticism unnerved Indra, king of the devas, who sent the apsara Alambusha to destroy Dadhichi's concentration. The nymph sported naked in the River Sarasvati just when the sage was performing his morning ablutions. The sight of the voluptuous nymph so captivated the sage that he lost control over his senses and spurted semen in the river. The river-goddess became pregnant with Dadhichi's child and in due course gave birth to the sage Sarasvata.

Mahabharata

Sexual desire does not always come in the form of a woman. When forcefully suppressed rather than smoothly sublimated, it can manifest itself in the most perverted forms:

The sage Vibhandaka controlled his senses, restrained his mind, and retained his seed in the hope of transcending the material world. His tapas disturbed Indra, so he sent the beautiful nymph to enchant the sage. Looking upon her, the sage was so overwhelmed by desire that he spilled his seed. The seed fell on grass that was eaten by a doe. In time the doe gave birth to Vibhandaka's son. He had a horn in the middle of his forehead and hence, he came to be known as the horned sage, Rishyashringa.

Mahabharata

Sometimes, a gentler temptation ensnares the sage within samsara:

King Bharata renounced the world, bridled his senses, and disciplined his mind. Just as he was about to attain moksha, he saw a tiger attack a pregnant doe. The doe escaped but eventually succumbed to her injuries. Just as she breathed her last, a fawn slipped out of her womb unnoticed. The sight of the helpless fawn aroused maternal instincts in Bharata's heart. He gave up meditating and began to look after the fawn. When he finally died, the last thought in his mind was of his pet fawn. As a result, he who was on the verge of liberation was reborn in samsara as a deer.

Bhagvata Purana

Such was the power of pleasure that fathers were willing the crush the joys of their children to hold on to it:

Yayati betrayed his wife Devayani and took her maid Sarmishtha as his concubine. When Devayani discovered this, she complained to her father, the sage Shukra, who cursed Yayati to become old and impotent. Yayati begged that his youthful vigor be restored, for he still lusted for worldly pleasures. "You can get your youth back if one of your young sons willingly accepts your old and withered body." Yayati went to his sons. None but the youngest, Puru, agreed to become old for their father's sake. As the years passed, Yayati realized that the thirst for worldly pleasures was unquenchable. Realizing the impermanence of earthly desires, he decided to renounce the world. He let Puru have his youth back and retired to the forest to live the life of a hermit and seek spiritual bliss.

Mahabharata

A true sage knows that worldly pleasure and worldly power, kama and artha, are ephemeral. They do not seduce him. He ends up seducing the seducer:

The sages Nara and Narayana isolated themselves in a cave to perform tapas. Indra sent all his apsaras to seduce them. The nymphs danced and sang, but the sages remained unmoved. They simply slapped their thighs. Out came a woman more ravishing than all the other nymphs put together. Her name was Urvashi. Overwhelmed by her beauty, Indra carried her off to Amravati and left the two sages alone.

Bhagvata Purana

Escape or Control?

Monastic orders reject the delights of the worldly life and, by extension, women. They are dominated by the Vedantic belief that material reality is a delusion, or maya, that tricks the senses and bewitches the mind.

A monk seeks the truth beyond appearances. He disciplines the mind so that it is not swept away by the allure of Nature. He understands cosmic mysteries and gains insights into the workings of the world. He can use the knowledge gained to practice *samadhi* and liberate himself from the cycle of life. He can also use it to acquire *siddhi* and manipulate the workings of the world around him.

The agenda of the nymph when she appears before the sage is twofold—to test his resolve for liberation and to obstruct his quest for occult power:

King Kaushika tried to steal the sage Vasistha's cow Nandini by force of arms. The sage fought back with the power of siddhi. He conjured up an army from thin air and defeated the king. Realizing that material might was no match for spiritual prowess, Kaushika decided to become a rishi and more powerful than Vasistha. He renounced his kingdom, left for the forest, and began practicing austerities. To distract him, Indra sent the apsara Menaka, who danced naked before him and succeeded in seducing him. When Kaushika realized how he had been tricked, he turned away from Menaka and resumed his austerities. Indra then sent the apsara Rambha. Kaushika had acquired enough control over his senses to resist Rambha's charms but not adequate restraint over his rage. With whatever spiritual prow-

ess he had gathered, he cursed Rambha to turn into a stone. Undaunted by his failure to control his mind, Kaushika resumed his austerities. Indra dispatched another set of nymphs, but this time Kaushika was beyond temptation or irritation. He had truly conquered his mind to become the great rishi Vishvamitra, renowned for his spiritual prowess.

Mahabharata

Menaka tempts the rishi sexually. Rambha goads him to violence. Either way, the apsaras succeed in making him speak the language of Nature and thus remain within the cycle of life. Sex and violence maintain the integrity of samsara. An organism indulges in sex for self-propagation and gives in to violence for self-preservation. Sex and violence fetter all creatures in the space-time continuum. Those who seek freedom from Nature do not speak this language; those who seek profit from Nature do. Hence celibacy and nonviolence form the cornerstone of monasticism, while sex and blood sacrifices are integrated in fertility rites.

The confrontation of the rishi and the apsara is not just the confrontation of this-worldly desires and otherworldly aspirations, it is also the confrontation of the fertility cults and monastic orders.

Fertility cults support materialistic aspirations—more crops, more cows, more children. Sex plays a vital role in it. Indra, god of rain, is renowned for his unrestrained libido because as lord of fertility his virility prevents famine and poverty. He strikes dark clouds with his thunderbolt, makes love to the earth-goddess with rain, and causes her to bring forth vegetation. Any attempt to oppose Nature's way threatens Indra. The lord of fertility cannot tolerate asceticism. His use of apsaras to weaken the resolve of rishis reflects the im-

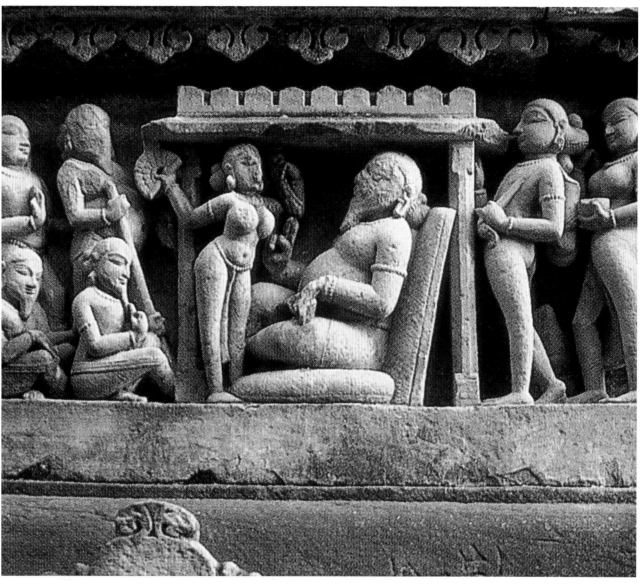

A courtesan, earthly representative of the celestial asparas, conversing with a sage.
Wall carving; Khajuraho temple, Madhya Pradesh. Twelfth century.

portance given to women in fertility cults.

As vessels of creative energy, the role of women is vital in all rites seeking to enhance Nature's life-giving capacity. These ceremonies are strongly influenced by the Tantrik belief that the feminine principle of life is shakti or the source of all power. Charms known as *yantras*, chants known as mantras, as well as ritual sex, or *maithuna*, are used to harness Nature's creative power so that the soil may be more productive and animals more fecund. In Hindu households the unwidowed matriarch is expected to wear bright clothes, color her hands, feet, and head with vermilion paint or powder, and adorn herself with jewelry and flowers. She is also expected to decorate the house with auspicious symbols and draw sacred diagrams called *rangolis* on thresholds to usher in good fortune. She observes fasts and performs rituals known as *vratas* to ensure the health and happiness of the household. She is called a suhagan, the unwidowed matriarch who harnesses the best things samsara has to offer. She plays out the traditional role of a priestess in a fertility rite:

Right from birth, Rishyashringa had been prevented by his father from looking upon a woman. He lived an ascetic's life in the forest, devoid of all sexual desire. In time he acquired siddhi. One day, when he was carrying a pitcher of water, rain fell in such torrents that his pitcher broke. Enraged, he used his spiritual powers to prevent Indra from releasing water from the clouds for twelve years. The famine caused havoc on earth. The only way to overturn Rishyashringa's curse was to make him lose his spiritual prowess. A local king, advised by the devas, sent his daughter Shanta to seduce the sage. Rishyashringa, who had never seen a woman, wondered who or what she was. Her strange body with gentle curves and alluring protrusions aroused his curiosity. Curiosity turned into attraction, then attachment. While his father was away, Rishyashringa expressed his desire to touch Shanta. She let him. Soon he was overwhelmed by desire. He made love to Shanta, spilled his semen, lost his control over the forces of Nature, and it began to rain.

Jatakas, Mahabharata

The shedding of semen—like the sowing of seed or the transmission of pollen to flowers by bees—enhances the fertility of Nature. Withholding semen goes against the cycle of life and generates energy that propels the ascetic out of samsara. This energy is tapas.

Semen Power

According to traditional Hindu physiology, semen is a magical substance, each drop of which is produced by a hundred drops of blood. The rasa in food transforms into plasma, then blood, then flesh, then fat, then bone, then marrow, then nerve, and finally semen. Semen is thus concentrated rasa, powerful enough to hold the spirit and pass it into the womb. When semen is retained, it turns into a wonderful substance called *ojas*.

Ojas seeps through the flesh and enlivens the body. It helps man think and feel. It can be used up by indulging the senses and reacting to worldly stimuli. Or it can be retained by reducing one's interaction with the world around. The aspiring yogi, rishi, or siddha shuts his eye, controls his breath, bridles his senses, disciplines his mind, and retains ojas, transforming it into spiritual fire, or tapas.

Tapas is the product of perfect mental and physical control. It generates an aura around the ascetic and makes him powerful. He can use this fire for samadhi, burn his karmas, shatter his ego, and break free from the cycle of life. Alternatively, he can use this power to attain siddhi and to manipulate the forces of the cosmos. Siddhi gives the adept the power to change the size or shape of his body, levitate and fly, acquire anything by will, control space and time, be blissful, and attain godlike status.

Only ungodly mortals shed semen:

The demon Jalandhara created nymphs to distract Shiva. While Shiva was thus distracted, the demon took the form of Shiva, entered Shiva's abode, and invited Parvati to make love with him. That Shiva had himself requested her company made Parvati suspicious. She asked her handmaiden Jaya to take her form and go to Jalandhara. Disguised as Parvati, Jaya made love to Jalandhara. He passion was spent and seed spilled in no time. "You who cannot hold your semen cannot be a god, let alone Shiva," said Jaya, "Begone and die."

Padma Purana

He who seeks samadhi or siddhi avoids contact with women. When he does embrace one, he does not shed his seed; instead he draws out female creative energy, the very essence of a woman's being:

In the hope of killing Shiva, the demon Adi took the form of Parvati, placed teeth sharp as thunderbolts in her vagina, and requested Shiva to make love to her. But Shiva recognized the imposter and made love to him without shedding his seed. Finally, unable to withstand the intensity of Shiva's lovemaking as Parvati could, Adi died.

Matsya Purana

Man's immortal soul comes from the father's seed and mortal flesh from the mother's menstrual fluid. Female creative energy is also destructive energy that fetters man to the cycle of endless rebirths. A man born without being tainted by menstrual fluid is therefore a superman possessing an ever youthful body and an all-powerful mind that is unaffected by the transformations of samsara. Such a man is called a *vira*.

Embodiments of Virility

A vira is both an ascetic and a warrior. As ascetic, he rejects women and the delights of worldly life. His mental control generates tapas, which gives him enormous physical strength. Thus, the asceticism of the vira is responsible for making him a warrior.

A vira is considered the embodiment of virility because he has no contact with women in his entire life. He is not even born of a woman:

The god Vishnu once took the form of the damsel Mohini. Enchanted by her looks, Shiva spurted semen. Vishnu collected the semen and transformed it into a child called Aiyanar.

Sabarimala Sthala Purana
from the state of Kerala

Also known as Ayyappa or Sastha, Aiyanar is the son of two male gods Shiva and Vishnu, hence a-yoni-ja, or nonwomb-born, untainted by menstrual blood. He is adopted by a childless king and raised as prince until the queen gives birth to a son and ambition rears its ugly head:

To secure the throne for her son, the queen feigned illness and claimed that only the milk of a leopard fetched by a virgin warrior would cure her. Sastha immediately set out for the

forest. While milking the leopard, tamed by his divine aura, he came upon a wild forest spirit, an ogress called Mahishi, who attacked him in the form of a female buffalo. Ayyappa killed her with ease and returned to the city seated on a tigress, covered with battle scars and bearing a pot of leopard's milk. The people cheered him and wanted him to be king. But Sastha refused the crown and returned to the forest. Accompanied by the warrior called Vavara, he had many adventures before he finally settled down atop the hill of Sabarimala.

Sabarimala Sthala Purana
from the state of Kerala

Sastha's image depicts him seated in a characteristic position of a yogi with a strip of cloth known as *yoga-patta* tied around his thighs to symbolize his firm grip over his mind and body. He has no interest in worldly life. He has no consort. Women are not even allowed to enter his shrine. His eternal companion is a male. His enemies—the ambitious queen and the wild ogress—are female. He thus triumphs over all things material, serenely transcends worldly emotions, and lives a life untouched by femininity, free from the cycle of life.

Conception without Sex

In Shiva Purana the semen spurted by Shiva aroused by Mohini's beauty is collected by the wind-god Vayu and poured into the ear of Anjani who eventually gives birth to the monkey-god Hanuman, not through her womb but through her side. Like Aiyanar, Hanuman is a celibate vira. Women avoid worshipping Hanuman because they respect his celibacy and do not wish even inadvertently to be a

source of temptation. Hanuman is a patron of wrestlers, who are also advised to remain celibate if they wish to acquire superhuman strength.

Interestingly, in Balinese Hinduism the monkey-god Hanuman is not quite the chaste warrior-god of India. He is quite a ladies' man who uses his sexual prowess to subjugate women and his physical strength to defeat men.

The *natha-jogis* of India worship Hanuman as the greatest of siddhas. Greatest because he has no ego and, despite his powers, finds validation in selflessly serving Rama, the noble prince of Ayodhya, the most august incarnation of Vishnu. Natha-jogis are monk-magicians who possess siddhi. They crave no worldly fortune, yet have the capacity to control the workings of samsara. They wander around the countryside telling tales of Hanuman's legendary celibacy, which gives him the power to father children without having sex:

Hanuman once had to go the netherworlds to rescue Rama from the clutches of the demon-king Mahiravana. An extremely powerful doorkeeper named Makaradhvaja blocked his path. Baffled at not being able to defeat Makaradhvaja, Hanuman used his siddhi to invoke the mother-goddess. The goddess appeared before the two warriors and revealed that Makaradhvaja was the son of Hanuman. "How can that be?" asked Hanuman. "I have never been with a woman." The goddess explained that long ago, when Hanuman was flying across the sea, a drop of his sweat fell from the skies right into the mouth of a sea elephant, or makara. His sweat was so potent that the makara became pregnant and in due course gave birth to Makaradhvaja. "Born of

your powerful bodily fluid, Makaradhvaja is as powerful as you, hence you are unable to defeat him," revealed the goddess. After hearing the secret of his birth, Makaradhvaja sought expiation from the sin of raising his hand against his own father. He helped Hanuman kill Mahiravana and liberate Rama.

Adbhuta Ramayana,
folklore from Uttarakhand

In another story the sound of Hanuman's voice could impregnate the women in the land of amazons:

Mainakini, princess of Sinhala, once saw a celestial spirit named Vasu flying across the sky. The wind pulled at his clothes and from down below Mainakini could see his manhood. She commented on its size and began to laugh. Enraged, the Vasu carried Mainakini to the land of amazons and left her there surrounded by women with no access to men. The land of amazons was a cursed site that no man could enter and no woman could leave. Sexually frustrated, the lonely women of amazon-land invoked the mother-goddess. The mother-goddess ordered Hanuman to help the women of amazon-land become mothers. "But how can I, a celibate warrior, make them pregnant?" wondered Hanuman. Rama came up with a solution. "Someone whose voice is as potent as yours does not need to have physical relations to make a woman pregnant." Accordingly, Hanuman went to the frontier of amazon-land and began to sing songs in praise of Rama. All the women who heard him sing became pregnant. They praised Hanuman's vocal virility.

Nava-natha-charitra

Though Hanuman succeeded in giving Mainakini a child, she desired physical pleasure with a man. For her satisfaction, Hanuman sent his disciple, the leader of natha-jogis, Matsyendra-natha to her queendom. Only Matsyendra-natha possessed enough spiritual prowess to survive in the land where no man was allowed to tread:

An embryo within a pregnant fish overheard Shiva revealing secret siddha techniques to his consort Parvati. With this information, the fish embryo transformed into a man. Shiva blessed this man and named him Matsyendra-natha, who went on to become first of natha-jogis. Hanuman ordered Matsyendra-natha to go to the land of the amazons and sexually satisfy Mainakini and all the women there. Matsyendra-natha did as ordered. As time passed, the carnal pleasures made him forget all about his life outside the amazon-land. Years later Matsyendra-natha's student Gorakshanatha entered the amazon-land and admonished his guru for losing control over his senses. Shaken out of his enchantment with worldly things, Matsyendra-natha bid farewell to Mainakini, put on his monk robes, and renounced the amazon-land forever.

Nava-natha-charitra

Matsyendra-natha's celibacy enables him to enter the land of women, but his carnality entraps him there. This folk tradition reiterates the classical belief that maya binds a person to samsara; tapas liberates him. Tapas is the spiritual fire that water-nymphs, the apsaras, seek to douse.

A Multilayered Cosmos

Semen energized by tapas, it is said, moves in the retrograde direction up the spine, pierces psychic nodes, and reveals to the mind the mysteries of the universe unfathomed by human minds. This knowledge makes man a *kevalin*, an omniscient being. The Jain Tirthankaras are all kevalins who have knowledge of the past, present, and future of all living beings. This knowledge helps them realize the ephemeral nature of all things. They break free from the clutches of samsara and rise to their heaven—abode of perfection—that stands beyond svarga, the celestial sphere of devas.

The Jain cosmos is multilayered. At the bottom is the realm of matter, the chthonian world, the world of flux, where everything is bound by the rules of space and time, where every idea is relative, every truth conditional, every event illusory, every mood transitory. On top is the spiritual realm—the paradise of eternal bliss, the abode of absolute reality, where everything is still and serene. According to Jain belief, he who sheds his attachment to material life floats to succeedingly higher planes of existence and ultimately reaches heaven. Those who are free from all attachments break free from samsara altogether and go to the heaven of the eternally blissful and all-aware Tirthankaras.

While Buddhists of old Hinayana school believe that their leader was a man who at the end of his existence on earth attained *nirvana* and ceased to be, Buddhists of the later Mahayana school came up with a multilayered cosmology, similar to the Jains, according to which the *buddhas* were not just enlightened mortals but godlike beings who lived in the highest heaven. The Buddhist heaven is a place of pure bliss; below are layers of increasing sensuality and sorrow.

In Hindu cosmology *lokas* are radiant, joyful realms located above man's head while *talas* are murky, morose regions located below the feet. Karma weighs down the soul with matter and binds man to earth. Destruction of karma provides man with the possibility of being reborn in a higher realm as a god and enjoying an eternity of endless joy. Accumulation of karma, on the other hand, dooms man to be reborn as an earthbound reptile or, lower still, in the nether regions, as a demon, eternally tormented by hatred, envy, desire, and death—the Hindu hell:

For the triple crime of having adulterous relations with a woman, killing a cow, and eating it, the king Satyvrata was cursed by his preceptor Vasistha to turn into an outcast named Trishanku. Being an outcast, Trishanku could never enter heaven. He decided to perform a yagna and override the fate thrust by Vasistha's curse. Only the sage Vishvamitra condescended to perform the ritual on behalf of an outcast. By the power of yagna, Trishanku rose to Amravati, but the devas kicked him out. As he tumbled down, Vishvamitra used the power of tapas and arrested his descent. Neither the devas nor Vishvamitra were willing to relent, so Trishanku remained suspended head-downward between heaven and earth.

Mahabharata, Harivamsa,
Devi Bhagvatam

In this story sex and violence—both involving females—prevent Trishanku from entering heaven. The use of yagna to earn merit and enter the city of the gods is a Vedic belief. In the post-Vedic period, as ritualism gave way to monasticism and mysticism, more and more Hindus came to believe that by the power of yoga—especially bhakti yoga, or the yoga of devotion—one could rise still higher and reach Brahma-loka, a realm where there is nothing but absolute truth, pure consciousness, and perfect bliss, *sad-chit-ananda*.

Each layer of the Jain, Buddhist, and Hindu cosmos could be seen as a metaphor for a state of consciousness. When the mind gets more and more attached to worldly things, one sinks deeper and deeper into the abyss of suffering. As the mind gets increasingly detached, one attains the state of unconditional joy that is heaven.

Fettered by Blood

Heaven is for men only. The devas who live in the Hindu paradise Amravati are all male. The only female residents of the Hindu paradise are apsaras, celestial courtesans, objects of divine pleasure.

In the Nepalese Mahayana text Svayambhu Purana *adi-buddha*, the primal being who resides in the highest heaven, is male, as are the *dhyani-buddhas* who surround him. Even the five *boddhisattvas*, mentally created by the *dhyani-buddhas*, who cast compassionate looks upon suffering beings, are male.

Twenty-three out of the twenty-three Tirthankaras of the Jain canon are male. Only one, the nineteenth Tirthankara—Mallinatha—is a woman. But her female body is a manifestation of imperfection:

✳

After completing worldly duties, King Mahabala and seven of his friends renounced the world and became Jain mendicants. They made a pact to take up identical numbers of fasts as part of their austerities. However, because of ill health, Mahabala could not eat all his meals. Thus he inadvertently fasted more than his friends and acquired more merit, enough to make him a Tirthankara in his next life. Because these merits were acquired by breaking a pact, he was reborn with the body of a woman and named Malli, "jasmine flower." Her beauty won her many suitors, who went to war over her. Malli was so disgusted by the carnage resulting from lust for her body that she turned her back on worldly life and became a monk. Eventually she became a kevalin and ascended to the paradise of Tirthankaras.

Jnatri-dharma-katha-sutra

The story of how Malli acquired a female body comes from scriptures of the Shvetambara, or white-robed Jains. The more austere Digambara, or sky-clad Jains, reject the very idea of Malli's womanhood. To them, Mallinatha was a man. They believe that a woman can never become an enlightened kevalin. The female physiology does not permit it.

Digambaras believe that a Tirthankara triumphs over all bodily needs and mental urges through wisdom and willpower. He rises above the mundane requirements of survival and hence acquires the capacity to transcend the chthonian cycles of birth and death. If Malli had a woman's body, he would not be able to do the same. As a woman, Malli may have been able to attain wisdom, overcome desire, rein in hunger, control breath, like any male ascetic, but she would not have been able to will her way out of menstrual tides. Escape from the wheel of the existence would therefore have been impossible. Menstruation anchors women to the earth, traps them in the chthonian realm. Possession of a male body is therefore a prerequisite for crossing the bridge to paradise. Besides, as a woman, Malli would not have access to the magical substance that catalyzes escape from worldly bonds—semen.

For a woman to attain salvation, Digambaras believe that she must first acquire a male body by living a chaste and exemplary existence as a woman. Thus, she is one step lower than man is in the spiritual hierarchy. Although Hindu scriptures do not express similar ideas so explicitly, the idea that a woman is more earthbound than a man is implicit in the Hindu worldview.

Woman is seen as the key to the wonders of samsara. These wonders—food and mineral wealth—come from below the earth. Thus aspiration for woman is aspiration for earthbound and not otherworldly pleasures. The apsara is associated with water, which always flows downhill; the rishi is associated with fire, which always rises skyward. In folk stories, when the mother-goddess appears on earth in the form of a baby, a priest or a king usually ploughs her out of the earth or finds her near a termite hill or in a lotus, that universal symbol of fertility. Virile male gods or viras, on the other hand, appear on hills and mountains, holding phallic spears, their heads touching the skies.

Termite hills are believed to represent the vulva, or yoni, of the earth-goddess. They mark the entrance to Bhogavati, city of lust, the abode of serpents. Serpents that crawl on the ground and regularly shed their skins as women shed menstrual blood know the secrets of the earth—how seeds germinate and where gems are located. Hence, they are powerful fertility symbols. Hindus seeking healthy children and good harvests worship nagas, or serpents, by pouring milk into termite hills. Also under the earth stands Hiranyapura, the city of gold, abode of asuras. These subterranean demons, enemies of the gods, are renowned for their architectural skills. Thus in sacred Hindu lore subterranean ungodly creatures such as nagas and asuras are linked to the delights of samsara—house, gold, gems, food, and yoni. The yogi in his quest for higher heavens renounces these earthbound foundations of worldly life:

Parvati, wife of the ascetic Shiva, wanted a home. But Shiva refused to be trapped within the four walls of a house. Said the wandering mendicant, "In summer, when heat blisters the skin, we will seek the shade of the banyan tree. In winter, when the cold is unbearable, we will seek warmth beside funeral pyres. And when it rains, we shall fly into the sky and live above the clouds." Thus did Shiva silence his wife's demand for a house.

Folklore from the state of Rajasthan

Women Saints

The association of women with worldly things does not mean that there are no women with otherworldly aspirations in sacred Hindu lore.

In the Vedic period, when ritualism governed society and man sought to harness rasa through yagna, the maiden Ghosha composed hymns invoking and adoring virile gods such as the Ashwini twins in the hope that they would ensure the potency of her future husband.

In the Upanishadic period that saw the rise of Buddhism and Jainism, when intellectual speculation on the nature of the divine principle reached a climax, one hears of female sages such as Gargi, whose sharp mind and tongue irritated many sages:

Janaka, king of Videha, dissatisfied with esoteric rituals, invited sages from all over the land to his kingdom and offered cows with gold-plated horns to anyone who helped him understand the true nature of the cosmos. Rishis, siddhis, yogis, all men attended the debate. Yagnavalkya dominated the conference with his view that reality is not the absolute truth and that yoga is the real yagna. During the proceedings, a woman walked naked into Janaka's court and introduced herself as Gargi. While all men looked at her body, it was with her mind that the woman astounded the assembled scholars. She asked Yagnvalkya on what is the foundation of water, the principle of life. "Wind," replied Yagnavalaya. And of wind? "Space." And of space? "Gandharvas?" And of gandharvas? "The moon." And of the moons? "The sun." And of the sun? "The stars." And of the stars? "The gods." And of the gods? "Indra." And of Indra? "Prajapati." And of Prajapati? "Brahman." And of Brahman? Exasperated by these unending questions, Yagnavalkya asked Gargi not to ask too many questions on that which is unfathomable lest her head fall off. Gargi smiled and declared that Yagnavalkya was the wisest sage in the assembly.

Brihadaranyaka Upanishad

Some women of this time preferred knowledge of the truth to worldly wealth:

Yagnavalkya wished to renounce the world and decided to distribute his wealth between his two wives, Maitreyi and Katyayani. Maitreyi did not want his worldly goods; she wanted him to give knowledge of that which never perishes—the Brahman.

Brihadaranyaka Upanishad

In the Epic age, when the Ramayana and Mahabharata were composed, Gautami accepted the vagaries of samsara with grace:

Gautami's son died of a snakebite. A hunter caught the snake and brought it to Gautami. "Let it go. Killing it will not get my son back. Serpents bite and people die. Such is the way of samsara," she said.

Mahabharata

Shandili did not appreciate being treated as a sex object:

Shandili was a pious woman who lived an ascetic's life atop Mount Rishabha. One day Suparna, the divine falcon-god, saw her and entertained the thought of carrying her away. Instantly, his golden wings dropped off. Suparana came crashing to the ground and begged Shandili to forgive him, because he did not seek to molest her. Shandili forgave him and restored his wings.

Mahabharata

In the Common Era the age of devotion known as the Bhakti age dawned, and many women saints appeared on the spiritual horizon. The steadfast devotion of these women to the divine principle despite all odds earned them the admiration and respect of society. One hears of Mira, the Rajput princess from northern India, who refused to acknowledge her husband as her true lord. When he died, she did not burn herself on his funeral pyre as tradition demanded of her. Instead she danced on the streets of Mathura and Vrindavana, singing praises of her divine lord Krishna. In southern India the daughter of a priest named Andal did not get married because her heart belonged to Krishna, her heavenly beloved. A woman's spiritual prowess scared off men, for they were used to seeing women as objects of worldly pleasure:

Punidavati lived in the village of Karaikal with her husband, Paramadatta, a seafaring merchant. She was so devoted to Shiva that the lord bestowed upon her magical powers. Her ability to conjure sweet mangos by merely wishing for them scared her husband who, after his next voyage, did not return home. Instead, he went to the city of Madurai, married another woman, and raised a family with her. When Punidavati learned why her husband had left her, she realized she had no more use for her beautiful body. By the grace of Shiva, she transformed herself into a crone with shriveled breasts and gaunt features so that no man could look upon her with eyes of desire. Thus she was free to devote herself to her lord. She became renowned as Karaikal Ammaiyar, the matriarch of Karaikal.

Peria Purana

Karaikal Ammaiyar rejects her body because she does not want to be attractive. Her behav-

Karaikal Ammaiyar, the woman who made herself ugly to follow the spiritual path. Bronze sculpture; popular craft from Tamil Nadu. Twentieth century.

ior is quite unlike male saints such as Bilvamangala, who restrains his urges as he begins his spiritual quest. She does not want to be seductive; he does not want to be seduced. Even among saints, man remains the victim and woman, the minefield of temptation.

Desire-Demon
or Love-God?

Woman attracts. Man is attracted. She is the stimulus that fetters man to samsara. She rouses desires that generate karma. Such beliefs caused the founder of Buddhism to hesitate while indoctrinating women into his monastic order. Then he saw the sorrowful face of his mother after the death of his father and changed his mind. Suddenly, he realized women were also victims of samsara, not instruments of Mara, the demon of desire.

Hindus know Mara as Kama. However, Kama is viewed as a god:

After the death of his first wife, Sati, Shiva refused to be part of worldly life. He isolated himself in an icy cave and immersed himself in meditation. But the gods wanted him to father a son who would be warlord of celestial armies. So they recruited the help of Kama, the god of lust. Kama flew into Shiva's cave on a parrot. His presence transformed the cold, lifeless cave into a garden for lovers, heady with the scent of spring flowers. Holding his sugarcane bow in one hand and pulling his bowstring made of bees with the other, he shot a flowery dart straight into Shiva's heart. When Shiva felt the palpitation of desire, he was not amused. With a detached ferocity, he opened his third eye and let loose a fiery missile that burnt Kama alive.

Shiva Purana, Devi Bhagvatam

Shiva destroys desire with the power of yoga in his bid to stay out of samsara. Without Kama, however, there is cosmic chaos. The bull does not mount the cow; the bees turn away from blossoms. There is no joy in pleasure gardens, as spring does not arrive. There is no love, no passion. Nothing rouses the flesh. Nothing inspires the rites of copulation. There is no conception, no rebirth. The wheel of existence grinds to a halt.

This is unacceptable to Vishnu, keeper of cosmic order, who in the Harivamsa is described as Kama's father. He understands the pain caused by desire but cannot ignore the importance of desire in rotating the cycle of life. He does not appreciate Brahma's lust, but does not agree with Shiva's asceticism, either. Vishnu stands between Brahma and Shiva. He neither creates nor destroys—he sustains. And to sustain the universe, the flow of spirit through semen and its embodiment in flesh is vital:

Shiva generated so much tapas that he transformed into a pillar of fire. The gods sought to release this bottled-up energy that could destroy the world. Meanwhile, the demon Taraka drove the gods out of Amravati. Only a six-day-old child could kill him. Such a child could be fathered only by Shiva. So the gods invoked the mother-goddess, who took the form of Parvati, princess of mountains. Because Kama could not make Shiva fall in love with her, Parvati decided to practice asceticism and through devotion earn Shiva's affection. Her austerities earned Shiva's admiration, and he embraced Parvati. The union resurrected Kama. Parvati gave Shiva's seed to Agni, the fire-god. But the radiance of the seed was unbearable. So the fire-god cast it into the icy waters of the River Ganga. The seed caused the river water to bubble. It set afire the reeds on the riverbanks. Amid the flames, the seed transformed into a six-headed child who was nursed by the six Kritika maidens. On the seventh day of its life, the child named Kartikeya let out a shrill war cry, grabbed a lance, and attacked and killed Taraka, thus restoring the reins of the cosmos to the gods. Kartikeya was declared the commander of celestial armies. Everyone saluted Shiva for fathering such a powerful child.

Shiva Purana, Skanda Purana

Shiva's excessive asceticism threatens the integrity of the cosmic cycle. Shakti domesticates Shiva, not with carnality, but through devotion. She makes him release his semen to help gods defeat demons and maintain harmony within the wheel of existence. Later she converses with him and patiently coaxes him to reveal the knowledge he acquired through aeons of meditation. This knowledge inspires the writing of the Vedas and the Tantras, books of mystical and occult wisdom, which greatly benefits humankind. She also inspires him to compose music and choreograph dance. Thus Shiva the ascetic becomes Shiva the artist. He begins participating in worldly life. The transformation helps samsara survive.

While Parvati tempers Shiva's asceticism, Sarasvati tempers Brahma's carnality. Sarasvati is the only goddess in the Hindu pantheon who is not associated with sex, violence, or fertility. Draped in a simple white sari, she holds books, musical instruments, and rosaries in her hand. She represents the serene wisdom, knowledge, and inspiration of Nature, beyond the bubbling fertility. She inspires scholars and artists to rejoice in rather than crave for the wonders of existence. She helps liberate man from the labyrinth of desire.

By giving Parvati to Shiva and Sarasvati to Brahma, Vishnu brings harmony between eroticism and asceticism, spirituality and materialism. He creates a middle path that offers liberation from the wheel of existence without disrupting the cycle of life.

Four Stages of Life

A balance between carnality and spirituality is necessary to harmonize this-worldly needs and otherworldly aspirations. So the Dharmashastra texts divided the life of the ideal Hindu man—*not* woman—into four stages. In the first stage, as brahmachari, he prepared himself to be a fruitful member of human society. In the second stage, as grihastha, he lived as a householder, raising children and fulfilling his obligation to his ancestors. In the third stage, as *vanaprasthi*, he gradually renounced worldly life and made way for the next generation. Finally, in the fourth stage, as sanyasi, he abandoned his wife, lived like a hermit, and sought the ultimate meaning of life.

Marriage was seen as a tryst with Nature: a time to fulfill biological obligations, a time to realize the ephemeral nature of worldly pleasures before moving on.

Before an ascetic began his spiritual journey, he was advised to fulfill worldly obligations:

Kardama wanted to renounce material reality and discover the spiritual truth. When he disclosed his intention to his wife, Devahuti, she requested him to give her a child before leaving. So he united with her without passion during her fertile period, fathered a son called Kapila, and then left for the forest.

Bhagvata Purana

Jain Tirthankaras also fulfilled worldly duties before renouncing the world:

King Rishabha taught men seventy-two vocations and women sixty-four skills. He established human civilization with the four orders of men. Such was his glory that Indra descended from the heavens and visited his court. To honor the king of gods, Rishabha invited the dancer Nilanjana to perform before his divine guest. Right in the middle of her brilliant performance, Nilanjana collapsed and died. Not wanting the performance to stop, Indra caused the corpse to disappear and conjured up an apparition to take the courtesan's place. The apparition looked and danced just like Nilanjana. No human eyes noticed what had transpired. No human eyes, that is, except those of Rishabha. "What is real—the apparition of Nilanjana that is seen or her corpse that is not?" wondered Rishabha. To find the answer, Rishabha renounced his kingdom and his crown and became an ascetic.

Jain lore

The ascetic who tried leaving the cycle of life without fulfilling his worldly obligations was sent back:

The sage Mandapala had performed tapas for many years. He had conquered his senses and had retained his seed in chastity. When he finally abandoned his body, he reached the land of ancestors and discovered that he had not received any fruit of tapas. On inquiry, he learned that a man who performs tapas but does not father children does not win the fruit of tapas. So Mandapala was reborn as a bird, and as a bird he made love to not one but two female birds and produced many children. Having thus fulfilled his biological obligations, he obtained the fruit of his tapas.

Mahabharata

A Lord of Enchantment

The ascetic who sought to obstruct the rotation of the wheel of life was penalized:

Prajapati Daksha, lord of civilization, created sons, and Brahma asked them to marry and produce children. When the celibate sage Narada told them about samsara, they refused to reproduce and broke free from the cycle of life. Daksha produced more sons and even they followed Narada's way of life. Enraged, Daksha said, "Don't you know, he who seeks release without paying his debts to the ancestors commits sin?" He then cursed Narada to wander aimlessly in the cosmos.

Shiva Purana

As if to make amends, the sage Narada becomes Vishnu's agent and works toward maintaining the integrity of the cosmic cycle. Lute in hand, he appears in sacred Hindu lore to stir up the plot, rouse the whimsical human mind with gossip, rumor, and suspicion. The resulting actions generate karma, and karma rotates the wheel of life:

It was foretold that Devaki's eighth child

would give birth to Kamsa's killer. Kamsa would have killed Devaki had her husband Vasudeva not promised to present their eighth child to Kamsa as soon as he was born. When Devaki was pregnant with her first child, Narada paid Kamsa a visit. "Congratulations on the conception of your killer," he said. Kamsa was puzzled by Narada's remark. "How do you know that Devaki has not gone through seven miscarriages before giving birth to this child? Do you think a father will willingly sacrifice his child so that you may live?" Narada's questions fueled Kamsa's anxiety. He decided to kill all children born to Devaki and Vasudeva. He threw the couple into prison and every time a child was delivered, he dashed the newborn against the stony floor. In this way Kamsa killed six of Devaki's children. When the seventh child was conceived, the goddess Yogamaya sprang out of Vishnu's heart. She transferred the fetus from Devaki's womb into the womb of Rohini, Vasudeva's other wife, who lived with her brother Nanda in a village on the other side of the river. When Devaki gave birth to her eighth child on a stormy night, Yogamaya cast the spell of sleep across the city of Mathura and unlocked the prison door. Instructed by the goddess, Vasudeva put Kamsa's nemesis in a basket and carried him across the river to the house of his brother-in-law and friend Nanda. Nanda's wife Yashoda had given birth to a girl-child that very night. Vasudeva exchanged the two babies and returned to the prison cell with Yashoda's daughter. The next day, when Kamsa grabbed the little girl, she slipped out of his hand and rose to the sky, taking the form of Yogamaya and shouting, "Kamsa, your nemesis lives far from your murderous gaze."

Harivamsa, Bhagvata Purana, Padma
Purana, Devi Bhagvatam

Yogamaya is the goddess of worldly illusion. Along with Narada, she successfully uses the power of imagination to terrorize Kamsa and drive him closer to the jaws of death. Instead of living a meaningful existence with the information at hand, Kamsa spends every living moment foolishly thinking of the future and trying to avert the inevitable. Such is the power of samsara on the human mind.

Yogamaya is born of Vishnu, who is the lord of all delusions. Vishnu uses the power of maya to make people participate in worldly activities. Using maya, he transforms himself into a nymph called Mohini, champion of worldly life.

As Mohini, Vishnu pours the nectar of immortality down the throats of the gods while distracting the demons with seductive smiles. Vishnu thus polarizes two sets of celestial beings, transforming devas into jealous guardians of rasa and asuras into eternal seekers of the sap of life. The resulting antagonism creates a force and counterforce that rotates the wheel of life. The triumph of the gods causes the day to dawn, the tides to rise, rains to come, the moon to wax. Their defeat at the hands of demons results in nightfall, the low tides, drought, and the dark half of the lunar cycle.

As Mohini, he also kills demons who try to create cosmic chaos:

Shiva, in his innocence, gave the demon Vrika the power to burn any creature alive by his touch. Vrika decided to test this power on Shiva himself. When he stretched out his hand, Shiva ran for cover. Vrika pursued him. Vishnu rushed to Shiva's rescue, taking the form of a ravishing damsel called Mohini. Enchanted by Mohini's beauty,

Vrika forgot all about the chase. "Can I hold you in my arms?" he asked Mohini. Mohini smiled seductively and said, "Only if you dance with me." "But I don't know how to dance," said Vrika. "Do what I do," said Mohini, who began dancing. Vrika followed her movements, moving his hands and hips as Mohini did. At one point Mohini touched her own head. Vrika, too bewitched by Mohini's charm to suspect a thing, touched his head, too. Instantly, he burst into flames. Thus did Vishnu use the power of maya to save Shiva from the demon Vrika.

Bhagvata Purana

As Mohini, Vishnu seduced Shiva, the greatest of ascetics, and ensured the flow of vitalizing semen into the cosmos. The sons born—Hanuman and Sastha—displayed Vishnu's world-affirming warrior traits as well as Shiva's world-renouncing ascetic qualities.

Desire, Duty, and Detachment

Vishnu enchants. He also liberates. But Vishnu's yoga is different from Shiva's yoga. Shiva's yoga is based on *vairagya*, or renunciation. Vishnu's yoga is based on bhakti, or devotion. While Shiva's yoga involves bridling the senses and controlling the mind to turn away from worldly pleasures, Vishnu's yoga demands disciplining the mind not to seek the fruit of labor. Shiva's yoga suits the ascetic. Vishnu's yoga is ideal for the worldly man. It allows him to be part of samsara while working toward liberation.

Bhakti redirects desire toward the spirit and takes this self-defeating emotion out of man's relationship with the material world. Dharma, or duty, not desire, becomes the motivating factor in man's association with samsara. Man participates in worldly life not to indulge the senses or inflate the ego but out of a sense of obligation to the cycle of life. His actions rotate the wheel of life but do not generate the karma that fetters the soul to the flesh. Thus is worldly order maintained and salvation guaranteed. This path is known as *karma yoga*.

When Shiva dances on Mount Kailas, he dances alone, detached from the wheel of existence that rotates around him. When Vishnu dances as Krishna, he interacts with the souls of all creatures, playing his flute, beckoning them to dance to the tune of this music. His tune is the tune of dharma:

The willful Krishna desired company. At once fair Radha came into existence from the left half of his being. As they made love, their delight gave rise to the colorful cosmos. As Radha perspired in the arms of her lord, innumerable gopis, or milkmaids, emerged from her pores. Each gopi desired Krishna's company and vied for his attention. So out of Krishna's pores emerged innumerable Krishnas. Each Krishna danced with a different gopi. Every gopi thought that the lord belonged to her and her alone. To teach them a lesson, Krishna disappeared. They were distraught and ran through the dark forest, maddened with grief. "Where is my Krishna?" they cried, and when they discovered their plight was similar to those of other gopis, they cried, "Where is our Krishna?" In response the lord reappeared, and the gopis were joyful. They formed a circle and danced round Krishna. Krishna picked up his flute and made music that delighted all.

Brahmavaivarta Purana

Radha comes into being because Krishna wills it so. She is fair; he is dark. She contains all colors; he is beyond the spectrum. Without Radha, Krishna is cheerless. Without Krishna, Radha is directionless. Krishna, the embodiment of spiritual reality, defies the law of space and hence is present at various places at the same time. He also defies the law of time and does not transform. Radha personifies matter. Over time her energy is parceled out into a multitude of individual manifestations—the gopis. Though born of the same Radha, ego makes every milkmaid think she is different from the other gopis. Ego also deludes them into believing that Krishna is theirs alone. As each form claims exclusive attention, there is discord and despair. Krishna disappears. Gopis are lost. Samsara is in disarray. When bhakti, selfless love for Krishna, resurfaces, Krishna reappears, harmony returns, and the drumbeat of desire is heard again.

Krishna's approach causes rasa to flow. When he departs, rasa ebbs. As rasa rises and falls, the cycle of seasons known as ritu appears in Nature. Ritu transforms Nature into a creature alive with many forms, a cosmic woman with many faces, each warm with passion, yielding her charms to her beloved who is lonely until she writhes in his arms. Krishna is the centripetal force, binding the women with his music. So long as all souls respect dharma, follow the tune, and stay in the circle, worldly delight and otherworldly bliss coexist.

Krishna in the center of the circle is param-atma, the universal soul, while Krishna with each of the milkmaids is jiva-atma, the individual soul. The two become one only when the milkmaids shed their egos and become one with Radha. This dance of Krishna in the circle of milkmaids is described as *rasa-leela*, the play of life.

Worshippers of Krishna identified themselves as diminutive doubles of Radha and, like her, they seek union with the lord. Longing was seen as a feminine emotion. In some bhakti subcultures, men even took to wearing female attire to get in touch with the feminine principle. They called themselves *sakhis*, or handmaidens of Radha. They crushed their masculine identities to become one with Radha and thus earn the eternal affection of Krishna.

As Krishna, Vishnu imbibed all the positive qualities of the love-god Kama while shedding the negative ones. Like Kama, Krishna is charming and delightful. The music of his flute, like the darts of Kama, rouses love and longing. Krishna enjoys the passion of moonlit nights and rain-drenched days. But while Kama inspires unrestrained pleasures, Krishna becomes the focus of ecstatic devotion. Carnal urges are elevated to spiritual longings. Affection is tempered with detachment:

As a child, Krishna played pranks on his mother. He raided dairies and stole butter from milkmaids. As a youth, Krishna played the flute, seduced women, and frolicked in the flowery meadows of Madhuvana on the banks of the River Yamuna. Then a time came when Krishna had to leave his rustic surroundings behind and enter the world of urbane politics. Without a moment's hesitation, he gave up his flute and his beloved Radha, and moved on to the next stage of his life to play the role of a warrior and statesman. He married the princess Rukmini and became mentor of the Pandava princes, guiding them to victory with force and guile in a great war at Kurukshetra.

Mahabharata, Harivamsa,
Bhagvata Purana

Women dancing in circles around Krishna as they perform the rasa-leela.
Rajasthani miniature painting. Nineteenth century.

Krishna loves Radha but leaves her when duty calls. He fights, he loves, he wins, he loses without getting enmeshed in the tangle of emotions. Unlike Shiva, who rejects samsara totally, Vishnu participates with detachment. He is neither erotic nor ascetic; he is romantic yet pragmatic, charming yet serene.

Nymph to Messenger

To many people there was something cold, insensitive, and aloof about holy men, who transcended worldly life and stood outside samsara. Many Buddhists found the idea of a buddha who abandons his suffering family on earth and rises to heaven for his own peace selfish and unpalatable. The transcendental principle seemed too detached from samsara to be capable of understanding the mundane sorrows of man. How could a man susceptible to worldly pleasures find comfort in the presence of one who had triumphed over the mind? Many sought a more compassionate and emotional alternative, and this manifested itself in feminine form:

Just as he was about to attain nirvana, Avatilokeshvara heard the cries of millions of suffering souls on earth. A tear rolled down his cheek and turned into the goddess Tara, the compassionate hearer of cries. Avatilokeshvara refused to leave samsara until all creatures on earth had attained salvation. He thus chose to stay behind as boddhisattva with Tara at his side.

Buddhist lore

Tara's heart warmed the cold rationality of Buddhism. She elevated the status of the female principle from nymph to messenger. The worldly man could approach Tara without feeling intimidated. In her arms, he could weep without restraint, confident that she would always comfort him. Her love was unconditional, her concern nonjudgmental. Because she embodied samsara, she understood his difficulties.

In Jainism too, each Tirthankara came to be attended by a goddess who helped man communicate his fears and insecurities to the heavenly seers.

The manifested female principle was more immediate to man than the disembodied male principle. In Nature man became aware of divine delight. Through body and mind, man could realize divinity. Matter was the medium through which the spirit could be reached. Though transcendent, the spirit acquired its divinity from the cycle of life. Hence, ascetic gods were often found embracing carnal goddesses, their shaktis, while expounding directive principles of monasticism:

The gods and demons went to the yogi Dattatreya to learn the secrets of the cosmos and found him embracing Laxmi passionately while she poured wine down his throat. The gods realized that Laxmi was Datta's source of power, his shakti, and that wine was the divinity she was bestowing upon him. The demons decided to abduct Laxmi and take her to the nether regions. However, without Datta, Laxmi's beauty and bounty bewitched the demons and made them weak and vulnerable.

Markandeya Purana

On her own Laxmi inflates the ego and deludes the mind with the allure of pleasure and power, kama and artha. But with Datta in the picture, her power is tempered and made benevolent. Around the finger of the divine, the wheel of life became less forbidding to the devotee. The goddess became the god's complement, not antagonist. She leads the devotee toward the divine.

Devotees of Vishnu saw his consort Laxmi not as the fickle goddess of fortune of the Vedic period, but as the mother of the cosmos who makes peace between the prodigal son and the divine father. To the devotee, wracked with guilt and shame for having succumbed to his ego and his senses, Vishnu, the awesome keeper of cosmic law, seemed too unapproachable and austere. He sought refuge in the more accessible maternal aura of Laxmi. She was heart, she was love, she was compassion. Through her he petitioned the almighty and sought moksha, release from the cycle of life.

Bhakti directs all desires to god. All actions become mere fulfillment of worldly obligations. Passionless fulfillment of dharma does not generate karma. The goddess can no longer seduce the flesh with the delights of samsara. The nymph becomes an expression of divine delight, a beautiful dream through which man finds his way out of the cycle of life.

CHAPTER FOUR

Cult of Chastity

SQUARING THE CIRCLE

Law of Civilization

In samsara sex and violence are unbridled. Only the fit survive. Nature is an impersonal web where all beings are locked in a never-ending struggle to stay alive. The hungry hyena will eat the pregnant doe. Sheep will trample over pretty daisies as they reach for that patch of succulent grass. There is no compassion, no hatred—only creation and destruction as the wheel of life rotates.

Society, or *samaja,* is an artificial construct. It is a space where man can liberate himself from the struggle for survival. He can transcend primal urges, explore art, and seek meaning in existence. Samaja offers choices that make man human. It is based on law that makes concessions for the weak. This law rejects nature's wild side, regulates instincts of sex and violence, domesticates Nature's fertility, and establishes civilization. Hindus call this law of civilization dharma. Dharma makes society stable.

Those who respect dharma are described in Hindu scriptures as *aryas,* "noble ones"; those who do not are equated with the wild forest spirits known as rakshasas. The rakshasas are despised because they cling to *matsya nyaya,* "law of the jungle," and oppose the ways of the aryas, especially their much-revered ceremony known as yagna in which Nature's benevolent energies are invoked and social interaction is promoted. The epic Ramayana is the tale of the confrontation of the aryas and the rakshasas:

Laxmana cutting off the nose of Surpanaka, the brazen rakshasa woman who dared to solicit him.
Chitrakathi painting; Paithan, Maharashtra. Nineteenth century.

Every time the rishi Vishvamitra tried to conduct his yagna in the forest, the rakshasas led by a female called Tadaka would attack and disrupt the ceremony. Exasperated, Vishvamitra sought the help of Rama, prince of Ayodhya, who was an incarnation of Vishnu, sustainer of civilization and upholder of dharma. Rama raised his bow and kept the rakshasas at bay. He was, however, unwilling to kill Tadaka because she was a woman. "It is not wrong to kill a woman to protect the weak," said the sage. So Rama raised his bow and shot down Tadaka.

Ramayana

Later, palace intrigues force Rama to leave his city and live like a hermit in the forest for fourteen years. His dutiful wife, Sita, and brother, Laxmana, follow him to the forest where, once again, Rama has to contend with the rakshasas:

Surpanaka, a rakshasa woman, saw Rama on the banks of the River Godavari in the Dandaka forest. Aroused by his beauty, she sought his amorous embrace. Rama refused to entertain her. "I have a wife already," he said. "Go to Laxmana, my brother, who is without one." Laxmana, who only wanted

to serve his brother, also turned down Surpanaka's proposal. Enraged, she decided to kill Sita and take her place by force. Laxmana stopped the wild forest-woman, cut off her nose, and drove her away.

Ramayana

As a rakshasa woman, Surpanaka follows the law of the jungle that does not recognize marriage. Like a flower, she attracts all bees. Like the forest floor, she accepts every seed. She expects all men to respond to her solicitations. But dharma does not endorse her free

ways. In Rama's realm marriage is sacred and infidelity a crime. Rama's hut in the forest marks an island of civilization. Across the threshold is wild Nature, where the weak have no defense, as Rama's wife, Sita, discovers to her horror:

Ravana, lord of rakshasas, was Surpanaka's brother. He decided to avenge her humiliation at the hands of Rama and Laxmana by abducting Sita. Sita's beauty, described by

Sita being confined to her house by a line drawn on the threshold by her brother-in-law Laxmana. Chitrakathi painting; Paithan, Maharashtra. Ninteenth century.

Surpanaka, played no small part in his decision. Ravana sent a golden deer and lured Rama out of his hut. Hours passed and there was no sign of Rama returning from the hunt. Fearing the worst, Sita begged her brother-in-law Laxmana to go and look for him. "Rama ordered me to stay and watch over you. But as you are forcing me to go, let me trace a perimeter around Rama's house with the tip of my arrow. Do not let anyone in. Do not cross it. No harm will befall you, so long as you stay within," said Laxmana before leaving. While the brothers were away, Ravana tried to enter Rama's campsite but discovered he could not cross the boundary marked by Laxmana. So disguised as a hermit, he called out to Sita and asked her to bring him some food. As the wife of a nobleman, Sita was obliged to feed the hungry. But Ravana demanded that she serve him outside the perimeter of Rama's house. "I cannot enter your house while your husband is away. It would not be proper. The least you can do, in keeping with the laws of hospitality, is bring out the food." Sita naively agreed to step out. No sooner had she done so than Ravana grabbed Sita and carried her to his kingdom.

Ramayana

By crossing the threshold, known as *laxmana rekha*, Sita steps into the world where might is right. She loses the protection conferred by dharma and pays the price. Hindus consider laxmana rekha the threshold of proper conduct. Every member of society is expected to stay within it. Rama, who sacrifices personal joy to stay within, is revered as *maryada purushottam*, "exemplar of rectitude."

Domesticating the Earth

In Tantrik art society is represented by a square circumscribed within a circle. The circle symbolizes samsara, acknowledging the fact that there are no sharp edges in Nature. Nature rotates according to ritu, the periodic ebb and flow of rasa. Sharp edges indicate human intervention, the unwillingness to go with the flow, the desire to hoard the sap of life and keep out the unwholesome side of Nature. Sharp edges mean dharma, the sharp edge of man-made law that establishes social order. Dharma decides what is acceptable in society and what is not. Dharma destroys the laws of the jungle and brings in the order of civilization. The process of domestication is a violent one:

The blind king Dhritarashtra decided to divide his kingdom to make peace between his hundred sons, the Kauravas, and his five nephews, the Pandavas. The undeveloped half, the forest of Khandava, was given to the Pandava brothers, who set out with their cows to establish their kingdom there. Krishna, their friend and guide, helped them in this endeavor. The fire-god Agni wished to consume the Khandava forest. But every time he tried, the rain-god Indra would rush to the rescue of the forest creatures, release water from the clouds, and put out the flames. Krishna and the Pandava Arjuna decided to help the fire-god. They invoked Varuna, lord of the sea, and obtained divine bows. Using these, they created a canopy of arrows over the forest that kept out the rain. Agni was thus able to enclose the forest with a wall of fire. Trapped by the flames, blinded by the smoke, the birds and

the beasts of the forest ran in every direction, crying out for help until they succumbed to the heat. Those that tried to escape the conflagration were hunted down by Arjuna and Krishna. When the fire had died out, the Pandavas built their city on the scorched forest floor. In the pastures around, protected from wild beasts by high fences, the Pandava cows grazed in peace.

Mahabharata

In another story that alludes to domestication of a river for the purposes of canal irrigation, the god of farming, Balarama, drags a river-goddess by the hair to satisfy his whims:

After consuming a great deal of wine, Balarama wanted to sport with women in the River Yamuna. He was too drunk to go to the river. He asked the river-goddess to come to him. The goddess refused to break her banks. So Balarama raised his plow, hooked the river-goddess with it, and dragged her to the orchard where he stood. The goddess writhed in agony and the river came to have many bends. Ultimately, she had no choice but to give into Balarama's wish.

Bhagvata Purana

Balarama, the farmer-god, tames a wild river into a canal, and Krishna, the cowherd-god, transforms a forest into a pasture. Both are incarnations of Vishnu, the keeper of worldly order. So is Rama, the destroyer of the rakshasas. Beside Vishnu, Laxmi is not the fickle goddess of fortune but a demure and subservient consort who massages his feet and serves him with affection. With dharma, Vishnu generates the square of civilization within the circle of Nature.

The women Tadaka and Surpanaka stand outside the square. They reject the fetters of civilization, with sex in the case of Surpanaka and with violence in the case of Tadaka. Sita's innate kindness makes her ignore the warnings of Laxmana and cross the line that isolates society from Nature. Yamuna refuses to willingly bow to Balarama's whim. These tales bring to light the Hindu belief that society is a demanding masculine organism called purusha while Nature is a stubborn female organism called prakriti. Prakriti needs to be domesticated by the laws of dharma for the sake of purusha. Thus did Hindu patriarchy justify itself.

Fathering Sons

In a patriarchal society producing a child is not enough to repay one's debt to ancestors. The child has to be male. A son is *putra*, deliverer from hell. He maintains the household hearth and offers funerary oblations to his forefathers. He is custodian of the family tree, keeper of family traditions, and inheritor of the family's spiritual line of descent.

A man who helps another man father a son earns great merit. One father goes to the extent of prostituting his daughter's ability to bear sons to earn merit for himself:

The sage Galava came to Yayati with a request for eight hundred horses to pay his fees to his guru, the sage Vishvamitra. Yayati had no horses to give. Not wanting to turn the sage away empty handed, he gave the sage his daughter Madhavi instead. "Oracles have foretold that my daughter will bear four illustrious sons. Let her bear one son for any king who will give you two hundred horses. When she

*will have borne four sons, you will have got
the eight hundred horses you want," he told
the sage. Galava took Madhavi around India
and she bore three sons for three kings, each of
whom gave Galava two hundred horses. No
other king had two hundred horses to spare.
So after giving six hundred horses to
Vishvamitra, Galava let his guru father a son
on Madhavi, a son who was worth the remaining two hundred horses. Later Yayati decided
to look for a groom for Madhavi, but Madhavi
rejected all proposals and preferred to become
a nun.*

Mahabharata

Traditional scriptures state that a son is
conceived when semen is stronger than menstrual fluid. Otherwise, a daughter is created.
If the male seed is as strong as the female fluid,
then the child born has both male and female
qualities—it is either a hermaphrodite or a
homosexual. To strengthen semen, Ayurveda,
the ancient Indian medical treatise, prescribes
continence, or brahmacharya; breath control,
or pranayama; exercises, or asanas; and a diet
of milk and milk products.

Other ways to ensure birth of a male child
include performing the ritual known as
putrakameshti yagna before the rite of conception to manipulate cosmic forces in one's favor. In the third month of pregnancy a sacrament called *pumsavana* is performed to ensure
masculinization of the fetus. During this now-
obsolete ceremony, juice of the banyan tree,
extracted by a virgin, was passed through the
right nostril of the pregnant woman, strength-
ening the *pingala*, or solar channel of her body,
that weakens menstrual fluid. The husband
would then place in his wife's palm two beans
and a barley stalk, symbolizing his genitals. He
would remove the grain from the barley stalk,
the semen, and hand them over to his wife in

the hope that it would strengthen the semen
in her womb.

Despite all this, if a man could father only
a daughter, tradition gave him the right to foster his daughter's sons as his own:

*The king of Manipura, Chitravahana, had
no sons. He had only a daughter who was
called Chitrangada. Chitravahana raised
Chitrangada as a boy. She grew up riding
horses, wrestling bulls, and hunting tigers.
One day she saw the Pandava Arjuna and
fell in love. Fearing that he would not appreciate her manly ways, she begged the gods
to transform her into a demure damsel. The
gods fulfilled her wish but Arjuna, used to
the attentions of beautiful women, ignored
her. When she learned that Arjuna had come
to Manipura to meet its much-talked-about
manly princess, she invoked the gods once
again and begged to be restored to her natural self. Her wish was granted and she rushed
to meet Arjuna, who instantly fell in love
with her robust mannerisms. He asked
Chitravahana for Chitrangada's hand in
marriage. "You can marry her only if you
forfeit all claims to the son she will bear. My
daughter's son should consider my lineage
as his own," said the king of Manipura.
Arjuna accepted the condition and married
Chitrangada. In due course they had a son.
He was named Babruvahana and declared
the crown prince of Manipura.*

Folklore based on Mahabharata
from the state of Bengal

Through sons, a man hoped to fulfill his
dreams. One father was so desperate for a son
that he refused to acknowledge the femininity of his female child:

Drupada wanted a son so badly that when his wife gave birth to Shikhandi he refused to acknowledge her as a girl. He treated her as a boy, raised her as a prince, and even got her a wife. On the wedding night Shikhandi's wife raised a hue and cry and informed her father, Hiranyavarma, the king of Dasharna, that her husband was no man. The indignant Hiranyavarma threatened to attack Drupada's kingdom with his mighty army. Drupada continued to insist that Shikhandi was a man but Shikhandi, confronted with the truth for the first time in her life, went to the forest to kill herself and save her people. In the forest she came upon a yaksha who offered to give her his manhood for one night. Shikhandi accepted the offer, went back to his city, made love to courtesans sent by Hiranyavarma, and proved his masculinity. In the meantime the yaksha's overlord, Kubera, cursed the yaksha to remain a eunuch forever, because he had misused his magic powers to part with his manhood. This enabled Shikhandi to function as a man for the rest of her natural life.

Mahabharata

When given a choice between a boy and girl, one king preferred to adopt the male child:

King Uparichara, while out on a hunt, spurted semen while resting on the forest floor. He wrapped it in a leaf and gave it to his parrot, instructing it to take the semen to his queen. As the parrot rose to the sky, it was attacked by a hawk, and the packet of semen fell into the sea where it was eaten by a fish. This was no ordinary fish, but a nymph called Adrika. In its body the king's semen transformed into two human children. When fishermen caught the fish, they were surprised to find a boy and a girl in its belly. They took the infants to King Uparichara, who adopted only the male child. The female child known as Matsya, the "fish-born," remained with the fishermen.

Mahabharata

The spurned illegitimate daughter of Uparichara—who is also known as Satyavati—so desired the royal destiny denied to her at birth that she married a king and made sure that the crown passed only to children borne by her:

King Shantanu fell in love with Satyavati and sought her hand in marriage. "Only if you make her sons your heirs," said her foster father. The king accepted the condition and told Devavrata, his son by an earlier marriage, to give up his claim to the throne. This did not satisfy Satyavati. "How can you guarantee that the sons of Devavrata will not fight for the throne?" she asked. For her sake, Devavrata took an oath: "I will never associate with women and so will never father a child." Only then did Satyavati marry Shantanu.

Mahabharata

By taking the vow of remaining childless for the sake of his father's happiness, Devavrata condemned himself to the hell called put. He therefore came to be known as Bhisma, "he who took the terrible vow." To delay his son's death, Shantanu bestowed upon Bhisma the power to choose the time he wished to depart from the land of the living. By a strange twist of fate, Bhisma died only because of circumstances arising from the vow:

Satyavati's sons were weaklings. One died before he could marry, and the other was incapable of winning himself a bride. So it was left to Bhisma to find wives for Vichitravirya, Satyavati's surviving son. He abducted the three princesess of Kashi— Amba, Ambika, and Ambalika—and gave them to Vichitravirya. When the oldest princess, Amba, revealed that her heart belonged to the king Salva, Bhisma let her go. However, Salva refused to marry Amba. "How can I marry a woman who has already been claimed by Bhisma?" he asked. Because women cannot go back to their father's house after leaving it in the arms of another man, Amba had no choice but to go back to Vichitravirya. Vichitravirya, quite happy with Ambika and Ambalika, was not prepared to accept a woman who had spurned him in the first place. Destitute, Amba begged Bhisma to restore her honor by marrying her. Bhisma, who had taken the vow of celibacy, refused to do so. "If you can abduct three women, why can you not marry one? If you have taken the vow of celibacy, why are you not in the forest living like a hermit?" Amba cried. Blaming Bhisma for her misfortunes, Amba went all around the world looking for a champion who would kill Bhisma and avenge her humiliation. No one, not even the warrior-priest Parashurama, could defeat Bhisma in battle. Finally, Amba swore to kill Bhisma on her own. She invoked Shiva, the god of destruction, who told her that she would be the cause of Bhisma's death in her next life. Unwilling to wait for death, Amba killed herself and was reborn as Shikhandi, daughter of Drupada, the king of Panchala. Years later Shikhandi managed to acquire the body of a man, meet Bhisma in battle, and be responsible for his death.

Mahabharata

Though fatally injured during the battle, Bhisma decided to use the power given to him by his father to delay his death until the sun began its northern, ascending journey after the winter solstice. The time chosen by Bhisma to die is significant. According to the Hindu calendar, when the sun is in its southern, descending course after the summer solstice, ancestors rise from the land of the dead to receive funerary offerings from their male descendants. Bhisma chose to die only after the ancestors had returned to the land of the dead. Perhaps he did not want to face his debtors. Because Bhisma died without issue, devout Hindus perform shradha in his honor on the day of his death on behalf of the male descendants who might have been but for his self-sacrifice.

Born within Society

Hindu dharma is based on the doctrine of obedience. All urges are to be disciplined to the demands of society. In ancient Hindu society women and men were expected to perform their social role without question. A woman's role as childbearer and homemaker was defined by her biology. A man's role was defined by his birth.

A man could take birth in any of the four primary castes, or *varnas*, of Hindu society. If born in the family of brahmanas, he became a member of the highest caste and had to take care of the spiritual needs of society. As a kshatriya, he had to take care of its political needs, while as a *vaishya*, he was responsible for its economic needs. If he was born in a *shudra* family, he became a member of the lowest caste and part of the labor force. According to the Rig Veda, the brahmanas, or priests and philosophers, make up the head of society; the kshatriyas, or noblemen and warriors, make up its arms; the vaishyas, or farmers, herdsmen, and traders, make up its trunk; and the shudras, or serfs, servants, and laborers, are the legs. Together the four castes keep purusha, the male organism that is society, alive.

In a world without society, fatherhood does not matter. All that matters is the fulfillment of male and female biological obligations to ensure the rotation of the cycle of life. How it happens, under what circumstances, makes little difference:

Satyakama wanted to study the religion of truth in the hermitage of Gautama. To gain admission, he had to name his father. "Of which seed am I fruit?" he asked his mother Jabala. Jabala replied, "I have known many men in my life. Go tell your teacher that you do not know who your father is but you do know that your mother is Jabala." When Satyakama introduced himself thus, the teacher was impressed, for the boy had taken his first step in the quest to learn the truth.

Chandogya Upanishad

However, within ancient Hindu society fatherhood mattered. A man's role was defined by birth. It was imperative that a man know of which seed he was fruit. A man without knowledge of his father was a bastard, unaware of his role in life. This was the tragedy of

Karna, one of the protagonists of the epic Mahabharata:

Kunti, daughter of King Kuntibhoja, served the sage Durvasa with great devotion when he visited her father's house. In gratitude, the sage taught Kunti a magic formula that would enable her to call upon any deva and have a child by him. Out of youthful curiosity, Kunti decided to test the mantra. She called upon Surya, the sun-god, who instantly descended from the sky and made love to her. The son, thus conceived, was born with a pair of divine earrings and a golden breastplate. Fearing a scandal, Kunti put the child in a basket and cast him to the whim of a river. A childless charioteer found the basket and raised the child as his own. Though raised as a charioteer, the sun-god's son who was named Karna showed all the qualities of a warrior. He befriended Duryodhana, prince of Hastinapur, and so impressed all with his skill in archery that he was made king of Anga. Despite his achievements, he was always taunted as a charioteer's son. All his life there remained a shadow in his heart—he did not know who he was, a shudra charioteer or a kshatriya king.

Mahabharata

It was almost impossible for a man to change the destiny determined by his birth, as one learns from the tale of the sage Matanga:

Matanga once hit a young donkey. The mother of the animal tried to console her offspring by informing him that nothing better could be expected of a chandala, *a low-*

caste undertaker. *Matanga, who came from a brahmana family, asked the mother donkey for an explanation. The mother donkey then disclosed that Matanga's mother had once, in a state of intoxication, made love to a shudra barber and that he was the product of that illicit union. Hurt by the truth, Matanga embarked on a course of austerities to obtain from the gods his promotion to the varna of brahmanas. His austerities won him the admiration of Indra, king of the devas, who offered him many boons but expressed his inability to change his caste.*

Ramayana

Union of Unequals

In a society defined by caste the union of a woman with a man from a lower caste was condemned by all: Such a *pratiloma*, or reverse union, led to a high-caste womb being contaminated by a low-caste seed. Ideally, women were expected to marry men belonging to the same caste. The marriage of a low-caste woman with a high-caste man, known as *anuloma*, was tolerated:

During a famine, the only person to earn a good living is the undertaker, or chandala, who tends to funeral pyres. During one famine, a group of starving sages went to the house of a chandala for food. But the chandala refused to serve them, fearing that by letting high-caste men eat in his house he would be breaking the code of dharma. He finally relented on the condition that Vasistha, leader of the sages, marry his daughter Akshamala. As father-in-law, it would be his duty to feed his son-in-law and

his friends, no matter what their caste. Vasistha agreed and married Akshamala. Akshamala's beauty overshadowed the radiance of the sun and so Vasistha named her Arundhati. In time Arundhati became renowned in the Hindu world for her wifely virtue.

Skanda Purana

High-caste men often had wives from different castes. However, the inheritance invariably went to the child whose mother belonged to the same caste as the husband:

By some quirk of fate, Gandhari was pregnant for two years. During this time, her husband, Dhritarashtra, took a concubine for his pleasure and she gave birth to a healthy and intelligent child named Yuyutsu. Though competent in every way, he could never be crown prince. That position was reserved for Gandhari's eldest son, Duryodhana.

Mahabharata

The status of the low-caste wife was often miserable. The author of the Aitareya Brahmana was the product of an anuloma union and had to face paternal discrimination:

Itara was a shudra wife of the sage Vishala. During a ceremony, the sage gave instructions to his sons by his upper-caste wife Pinga, but ignored Itara's son, Aitareya. Hurt, Itara told Aitareya to seek instruction from Mahi, the earth-goddess, who treats people of all castes equally. The earth-goddess instructed him for twelve years and he became renowned as Mahidasa, "servant of the earth-goddess." He

lived for over a hundred years and wrote several sacred texts.

Aitareya Brahmana,
Skanda Purana

In samsara childbearing was essential to rotate the wheel of life. In samaja childbearing had many social implications, making fatherhood vital for the survival of purusha.

Woman to Wife

Only when a man is convinced that a woman is sexually faithful to him can he believe that the child borne by her is the fruit of his seed. Considering the importance of paternity in ancient Hindu society, a woman could not claim that a particular man was the father of her son without adequate proof:

During a hunt, King Dushyanta chanced upon the lovely Shakuntala all alone in the hermitage of her foster father, the sage Kanva. His passions roused, Dushyanta suggested that they marry as the gandharvas do, without social endorsement. Shakuntala, attracted by the virile king, gave her consent. Without waiting for Kanva's approval, the two made love freely, outside the norms of society. His lust satisfied, Dushyanta left for his city, promising to send for Shakuntala as soon as it was possible. Years passed. Dushyanta did not return. Meanwhile, Shakuntala gave birth to a son whom she named Bharata. When the son came of age, he demanded to see his father. So Shakuntala took him to Dushyanta's court. Dushyanta was furious when she identified him as the

father of her son. "How dare you say that, you low-born wench," he said. He ordered her to leave his palace or stay behind as a concubine, for she was unworthy of being a queen. Hurt and humiliated, Shakuntala turned around and began walking out of the palace. Suddenly, a heavenly voice spoke up and told the royal court that Shakuntala was no liar and that the child she had borne was indeed the son of Dushyanta. Hearing these words, Dushyanta was overjoyed. "This divine testimony enables me to publicly acknowledge Bharata as my son. Now my subjects will not dare cast aspersions on your character and his paternity."

Mahabharata

In society witnesses are required who can testify to the union of man and wife. This makes marriage mandatory. In samsara women are adored as mothers who bring forth life. In samaja they are respected only if they are wives. Motherhood without matrimony is not appreciated. Matrimony harnesses female fertility. Women bear children for husbands, not Nature. The transformation of nymph to wife, of forest into field, is brought out in the tale of Marisha:

The rishi Kandu restrained his senses and retained his bodily fluids to escape the cycle of life. To distract him from his tapas, Indra sent down the apsara Pramlocha, who successfully managed to seduce the sage. In her arms Kandu found so much passion that a hundred years passed as if it were one night. When Kandu awoke from this erotic trance, he was furious and he ordered Pramlocha to go away. As she rose to the sky, trees brushed off her perspiration. Pramlocha was preg-

CULT OF CHASTITY ◆ 97

nant with the seed of Kandu at this time, and the embryo permeated from her womb through her sweat into the trees. The wind gathered the fluid embryo from the leaves, and moonlight transformed it into a beautiful girl called Marisha. She was Nature's daughter. Meanwhile, the ten Prachetas brothers were meditating under the sea. Their austerities gave them miraculous powers. When they came up after ten thousand years, they found earth uninhabitable, overgrown with trees. So they spat out fire, torched the forests, and cleared the land. To make peace, Nature gave the brothers Marisha's hand in marriage. Marisha, wife of the ten Prachetas, gave birth to Prajapati Daksha, lord of civilization.

Vishnu Purana

A Woman with Many Husbands

Marisha's marriage to ten men suggests that polyandrous marriages were perhaps part of Hindu society in ancient times. Marisha was not the only woman to have more than one husband simultaneously. There was Jatila who had seven husbands, and Varkshi who had ten. The most famous polyandrous woman of sacred Hindu lore was Draupadi, heroine of the epic Mahabharata, common wife of the five Pandava brothers:

The Pandava Arjuna won the hand of Princess Draupadi of Panchala after winning an archery competition. "Look at the prize I won at the contest," he shouted when he reached home. His mother, busy in the kitchen, spoke without turning around, "Whatever it is, share it with your brothers." Arjuna, who always

obeyed his mother, was therefore forced to share his wife with his four brothers.

Mahabharata

Bards and scholars have constantly tried to "explain" Draupadi's polyandrous status. The need to explain a woman's, but not a man's, polygamy is a symptom of a patriarchal society:

In her previous life Draupadi had pleased Shiva with her devotion, and he had offered her a boon. She asked for a husband who would be noble, strong, brave, handsome, and wise. "So be it," said Shiva. She thought that she would get a husband with these five qualities. Instead Shiva, the guileless god, in his innocence, had granted her five husbands, one noble, one strong, one brave, one handsome, and one wise.

Devi Bhagvatam

In many Puranas it is said that Draupadi was in fact an incarnation of the earth-goddess, while her five husbands embodied the five aspects of Indra, god of the sky. Another story suggests that Draupadi's polyandry was not a boon but a curse:

Nalayani was given in marriage to an old and frail sage called Maudgalya. The sage was only interested in austerities and never paid any attention to her. Still she served him as a dutiful wife. In time the sage contracted leprosy, but Nalayani continued to serve him. Pleased with her devotion, the sage offered her a boon. "Give up your ascetic ways and make love to me," she said. The sage instantly transformed into a young

man and embraced her. After many years, the sage decided it was time give up the pleasures of conjugal life. When Nalayani objected, the sage cursed her that in her next life she would be reborn as Draupadi and have five men who would satisfy her lust.

Folklore from southern India

Sharing a common wife led to fatal sexual rivalry between brothers, according to the sage Narada, who narrated the following story to the Pandavas to make his point:

Together the asura brothers, Sunda and Upasunda, were invincible. To drive a wedge between them, Indra, king of the devas, sought the help of the nymph Tilotamma. Both asuras fell in love with this apsara. Intoxicated by her charms, unwilling to share her beauty, they began fighting over her. The two were evenly matched and ended up killing each other, much to the satisfaction of the gods.

Mahabharata

The tale of Sunda and Upasunda made the Pandavas realize how a common wife could either bind them together or split them apart. It prompted them to make elaborate bedroom arrangements with Draupadi:

The five brothers decided to share Draupadi in rotation. She would cohabit with one brother exclusively for a period of one year. During this time, the other brothers would not enter her bedchamber or demand her company. At the end of each year, before letting the next brother share her bed, she

would walk through fire and regain her virginity. Thus each brother got the chance to deflower Draupadi and father a son in her. Once Arjuna, the third Pandava, entered Draupadi's bedchamber in search of his bow while Draupadi was with Yudhishtira, the eldest. For this transgression, he was exiled for twelve years.

Mahabharata

Draupadi's bedroom arrangements took care of sexual rivalry between the brothers. They also ensured that there was no confusion about the paternity of her five sons.

Social and Biological Fathers

Biological paternity was not always important in Hindu society. There was a time when fatherhood was more of a social issue. Man was father of his wife's children, whether or not they were fruits of his seed. Memory of this period is retained in many folktales:

When the merchant died, his relatives did not allow his widow to inherit his property. Destitute, the vaishya woman left the city with her daughter. As she made her way through her forest with her young daughter, she came upon a robber who had been impaled on a stake by a local king. The robber, who was on the verge of dying, told the widow, "Give me your daughter's hand in marriage and I will tell you where I have hidden all the gold I have stolen. As her husband, I will be the father of all her children and thus be able to repay my debt to my

ancestors." The penniless widow accepted the robber's offer. Soon after marriage, the robber died. The widow found the gold and settled in a nearby village, where her daughter fell in love with a priest. In due course she gave birth to her son, whom the oracles said would grow up to be king. To facilitate the process, the widow abandoned the child on the gates of a palace where lived a childless king. The king raised the foundling as his own. Years later the widow's grandson became king and performed a shradha ceremony in honor of his ancestors. As he was about to throw the oblation into the river, three hands sprang up to catch it—one was the hand of the robber who had married his mother, one the hand of the priest who had fathered him, and one the hand of the king who had raised him. The priests advised the king to offer the oblation to the robber who had married his mother.

Vetalapanchavinsati

Marriage made man master of his wife's womb. Like the owner of the field, the husband had full right over the harvest, irrespective of who sowed the seed. This claim over the womb did not expire with his death:

Vichitravirya died before he could impregnate his two wives, Ambika and Ambalika. So his mother, Satyavati, called upon her stepson, Bhisma, to impregnate the two widows. He refused because he had taken the vow of celibacy. So Satyavati sent for the sage Vyasa, her son born before her marriage, and asked him to do the needful. In due course, Ambika gave birth to a blind child who was named Dhritarashtra. Ambalika gave birth to a pale, sickly child

who was named Pandu. To produce a healthier child, Satyavati forced Ambika to sleep with Vyasa again. Unwilling to lie with the sage, Ambika asked her maid, the palace concubine, to lie on the bed. The concubine bore a healthy child who was named Vidura. Though wiser and stronger than his brothers, Vidura could not be king because he was the son of a concubine, not a queen.

Mahabharata

Society could witness only the marriage ceremony, not the ritual of conception. Consequently, society recognized only the man who married the woman as the father of her children. Even the gods gave social paternity more importance than biological paternity:

The star-goddess Tara was given in marriage to Brihaspati, the wise lord of the planet Jupiter. But she eloped with the handsome moon-god Chandra. Brihaspati, who was also preceptor of the devas, refused to perform sacrifices for the gods unless they brought his wife back. Some of the devas sided with the lawfully wedded husband, others sided with the lover. After a great war, Tara was finally restored to Brihaspati. She came with child, and both Brihaspati and Chandra claimed the fetus. Only Tara knew the truth, but she refused to speak. But when the unborn child, Budha, lord of the planet Mercury, demanded to know his origins, Tara revealed that her child was the fruit of Chandra's seed. Nevertheless, the gods declared Brihaspati, not Chandra, to be the real father of the child.

Bhagvata Purana

Perhaps the gods did not trust a woman's word. Perhaps the gods preferred law to love.

Whatever be the case, sexual fidelity was clearly not a subset of marriage until the sage Shvetaketu imposed monogamy on women:

During a great sacrifice, many sages visited the hermitage of sage Uddalaka. Uddalaka's son Shvetaketu noticed that his mother was in the arms of one of the guests and that his father was not particularly perturbed by her behavior. "Women, like men, are born free," his father explained. But Uddalaka's words did not quell Shvetaketu's outrage. He decreed, "Henceforth, women shall be faithful to their husbands and shall do as their husbands tell them to. Men shall respect chaste wives. Those who fail to do so will incur the sin of abortion." Since then, women have been expected to be faithful to their husbands.

Mahabharata

Shvetaketu's law gave the reins of a woman's fertility to her husband. He became the farmer who fences the field, pulls out the weeds, and chooses which seed to sow. Thus, social paternity became biological paternity.

The Man with Many Wives

Shvetaketu's law could easily be applied in monogamous households. In polygamous households, things were more complex. A woman with many husbands, such as Draupadi, had to make elaborate arrangements to make sure that only one husband shared her bed during a fertile period. Things were a bit simpler for a man with many wives. He had to ensure only that he visited each of his wives during her fertile period. If he did not, he could get into trouble:

Chandra, the moon-god, had married twenty-seven star maidens, daughters of Prajapati Daksha, but he preferred only the company of Rohini. He spent all his time with her. As a result, every night was a full-moon night. The neglected wives complained to their father, who warned Chandra to change his ways. When Chandra did not, Daksha cursed him with the wasting disease. As the days passed, his luster waned. To save himself, the moon-god sought refuge on Shiva's head and began to wax. Finally, an arrangement was made that compelled Chandra to visit each of his wives once a month. It is said that when the moon-god approaches Rohini, he waxes; when he moves away from her, he wanes. When he is without a wife, it is the new-moon night.

Skanda Purana,
Somanatha Sthala Purana
from the state of Gujarat

A polygamous husband could not always keep his many wives happy. Things sometimes did go drastically wrong in the women's quarters of a polygynous household:

Krishna, lord of Dwarka, had eight wives. When he defeated the demon Naraka, he discovered 16,100 captive women in Naraka's harem. To save the women from destitution and infamy, Krishna accepted them as his junior wives and took them to his palace. Krishna used his powers and

multiplied his body 16,108 times to be with all of his wives at the same time and to please them equally. Despite this, some of the junior queens turned their amorous attentions toward Samba, one of Krishna's many sons who was as handsome as his father. One woman named Nandini even took the form of Samba's wife and tricked her stepson into embracing her. When Krishna learned of these incestuous encounters, he cursed Samba with a skin disease. Samba had to propitiate the sun-god before he was cured of the condition.

Varaha Purana, Skanda Purana,
Bhavishya Purana

Sex Hospitality

Shvetaketu's law prevented women from choosing the seed they wanted sown in their womb. They could only choose husbands, who in turn selected the seed. If a wife was barren, she could always be replaced. But if the husband was impotent or sterile, Shvetaketu's law gave him the right to order his wife to go to another man and have children by him. As lord of the field, he still had right over the harvest, so long as he chose the seed. Many childless kings took advantage of this legally sanctioned levirate:

Pandu had two wives, Kunti and Madri. But a curse prevented him from making love to either of them. If he tried, he would die. Pandu ordered his wives to bear sons by other men for him. Kunti had a magic formula, or mantra, by which she could call upon the gods and have children by them. She used it three times, called three gods, and gave birth

to three sons. She refused to use the mantra again as, it was said, a woman who cohabited with more than four men was a prostitute. Pandu, who wanted more sons, asked Kunti to use the formula in Madri's name. Kunti obeyed her husband and gave the formula to Madri for a single use. Madri cleverly invoked the celestial Ashwini twins and had two sons by them. Kunti refused to let Madri use the mantra again because she feared that Madri would use the formula to invoke another pair of twin gods and thus bear more sons than she.

Mahabharata

Pandu's wife Kunti refuses to call upon more than three gods because according to her, association with more than four men makes a woman a prostitute. This belief perhaps explains why in the modern Hindu marriage ceremony, the bride is first given in marriage to the god of vegetation, Soma, then to the gandharva Vishvavasu, and finally to the fire-god Agni before she is given to the groom. Soma enjoys a woman when hair appears on her pubes, Vishvavasu has her when her breasts start to show, and Agni embraces her when she has her first period. By this metaphorical union to three divinities and then one human being, the Hindu bride uses up her quota of four husbands and thus is forbidden to remarry.

Shvetaketu's law permitted women to have sex with other men, provided their husbands willed it. This enabled husbands to share their wives with other men:

Sudarshana told his wife Oghavati that she should look after every need of his guests. Once, while he was away, the lord of social virtue, Dharma, decided to test Oghavati. He

came to her house disguised as a hermit, and Oghavati welcomed him in. "How can I serve you?" she asked. "By offering yourself to me," replied the hermit. In keeping with her husband's wishes, Oghavati gave herself to the hermit. While he was making love to her, Sudarshana returned home. He called out to his wife. "She is busy making love to your guest," shouted the hermit from inside the bedchamber. "Please carry on. Forgive me for interrupting," said Sudarshana. Dharma blessed the couple, pleased with Sudarshana's hospitality and Oghavati's obedience.

Mahabharata

In the above story Dharma, god of social virtue, endorses the practice of sex hospitality. Oghavati does not lose her chastity, because she did what her husband had asked her to. Sharing a wife with other men was seen as the sign of ultimate selflessness, which was much appreciated by the gods:

Disguised as a mendicant, Shiva sought shelter in the house of a hunter in the middle of the forest. But in the hut there was space for only two people. The hunter let Shiva sleep in the house with his wife while he slept outside. At night wild animals attacked and killed the hunter while Shiva slept in the hut in the arms of the hunter's wife. In the morning the hunter's wife mourned her husband's demise but was glad he died while upholding the laws of hospitality.

Shiva Purana

Not all women tolerated being treated as commodities. There were women who questioned the right of a husband over his wife's body:

Yudhishtira, the eldest of the five Pandavas, was invited to a game of dice by his paternal cousins, the Kauravas. Shakuni, maternal uncle of the Kauravas, played on behalf of his nephews and skillfully maneuvered the die so that Yudhishtira lost every game. As Yudhishtira lost game after game, he gambled away his kingdom, his four brothers, even his own self. Finally, he gambled away their common wife, Draupadi. Draupadi was dragged out of the royal women's apartments by the hair and brought to court. The queen, who had never been seen in public before, was treated like a common slave. Outraged, Draupadi asked, "Can a man who has lost himself wager his wife?" To this question, one man replied, "When Yudhishtira wagered himself, he effectively wagered all his property, and that includes you."

Mahabharata

Virtue of Obedience

The ideal wife, according to scriptures, is one who does household chores like a servant, gives counsel like a minister, is as beautiful and charming as the goddess Laxmi, is as patient as the earth-goddess, bestows love and tenderness like a mother, and gives pleasure like a courtesan. She subsumes her personality to her husband. She is undemanding in good times and supportive in bad times:

King Harishchandra once disturbed the penance of the sage Vishvamitra. To make amends, he gave the sage his kingdom as a

The goddess Laxmi massaging her consort Vishnu's tired feet, thereby expressing her subservience and domestication. Temple wall carving; Dasavatara, Deogarh. Sixth century.

gift. The sage accepted the kingdom as charity. Having lost his kingdom, Harischandra was forced to leave his city and live in the forest. As he left, his dutiful wife, Chandravati, followed him with their son. They had not gone far when Vishvamitra came after them demanding dakshina, *a monetary gift that must accompany any charity. Having given up his kingdom, the king did not have any money. He decided to raise the money by selling himself. "Sell me, too," said the virtuous Chandravati. So Harishchandra sold himself and his wife in the slave market and collected enough gold to pay Vishvamitra's dakshina. This act of integrity earned great merit for Harischandra. His wife became renowned for her conjugal devotion.*

Devi Bhagvatam

When the husband spent time with a prostitute, a good wife did not protest, just waited for his return patiently:

The merchant Kovalan spent all his time with the courtesan Madhavi. His wife, Kannagi, waited for him at home, with tears in her eyes, observing fasts and propitiating gods that he may return. When he returned, having squandered all his wealth on Madhavi, she accepted him with open arms. Kovalan could not bear to live in the city where he had lost his money and his reputation. He decided to travel to the city of Madurai and start afresh. Kannagi accepted his decision and silently followed him through the dark, dense forest, earning the reputation of the loyal and virtuous wife.

Shilappadikaram

Whatever the fault of a husband, the wife had to accept him unconditionally:

Surasena, king of Pratisthana, had a son named Nageshvara who had the body of a snake. The king concealed this fact and tricked Bhogavati, princess of Anga, into marrying him. When Bhogavati learned the truth, she accepted her fate and served her serpent husband with devotion. Later Nageshvara learned that he had been cursed to have the body of a seprent because he had overheard a secret conversation between Shiva and Parvati. His human body would be restored if his virtuous wife took him to a holy lake and gave him a bath. Bhogavati did as her husband requested, and Nageshvara regained his human form.

Brahma Purana

Clever Adulteresses

Ordering a wife to be chaste did not ensure her fidelity because, by nature, women were believed to be nymphs who derived much more pleasure from sex than men and hence had a greater appetite for it:

Bhangashvana had fathered many sons. Once Indra cursed him to become a woman. As a woman, he produced many sons. Thus, he had two sets of sons—those who called him "Father" and those who called him "Mother." Indra caused the two sets of children to fight and kill each other. When Bhangashvana pleaded for mercy, Indra asked which set of

sons he would like back. "Those who call me 'Mother,'" said Bhangashvana. When asked whether he wanted a male body or a female one, he replied, "A female one, so that I can get more pleasure."

Mahabharata

The idea that women are oversexed because they derive greater pleasure than men during sex is popular among many Indian tribes:

The first man and first woman stayed away from each other for sin of incest. The goddess of smallpox scarred their faces. Unable to recognize each other, they got married. However, they did not know how to produce children. So god gave them love charms; woman took more love charms than man and so women are more lusty than men.

Central Indian tribal lore

One erotic manual, the Koka Shastra, was written for the sole purpose of enabling husbands to satisfy their wives adequately so that they would not want to be with other men:

A woman once entered a king's court without any clothes on. When asked to explain this immodest behavior, she looked at the crowd of courtiers and declared scornfully that it did not matter because there were no men around her. "O King, not a single man in your kingdom has been able to satisfy me. My body burns with desire and the heat is unbearable. If I am walking around naked, it is because of your inadequacy. I challenge you to provide me one lover who will pleasure me adequately." The king hung his head

in shame when one of his courtiers, a brahmana called Koka Shastri, walked up to him and requested permission to take the oversexed woman home. "I know how to satisfy and silence her," he said. Koka took the woman home and spent the night making love to her so persuasively that before dawn, the woman was quite near fainting from fatigue and from repeated orgasms. She begged the brahmana to stop. The next day Koka dragged the woman back to the king's court and forced her to inform the king of her sexual subjugation by one of his subjects. She then solemnly covered her body in his presence. The king, anxious to learn how Koka had defeated the naked woman, commanded Koka to write a treatise that would teach all men how to satisfy their wives so that they might not run around naked.

Folktale from northern India

In the Garuda Purana one learns, "A woman has twice a man's desire for food, four times his cunning, and eight times his appetite for sex." This led to the popular belief that most women indulged in adultery but were just too cunning to get caught. The clever adulteress is a popular character in Indian folklore. The following story occurs in the Panchatantra, a book written by a priest who wished to impart worldly wisdom to his royal students:

A chariot maker returned home to find his wife's paramour in bed. He slipped under the bed hoping to catch his wife red-handed. When his wife walked into the room, she caught sight of her husband hiding under the bed. Rather than getting flustered, she began thinking of ways to outwit him. She be-

gan to cry and when her paramour tried to comfort her, she said, "I know I invited you into my house. You must think that I am a woman of loose morals. But you see, sir, I had no choice. The goddess appeared in my dreams and informed me that my husband will die within six months unless I go to bed with another man. That is the reason why I have invited you here. I know this is not right and that I shall suffer in hell for this, but that suffering is nothing compared to the pain of losing a husband. Will you help me save my beloved lord, kind sir?" The paramour realized that something was afoot and, with secret laughter lighting up his face, said, "Yes, noble lady, I shall do what you ask me and take upon me the sin of touching a chaste woman so that you do not become a widow." The fool of a husband was so pleased with his wife that after her paramour had finished making love to her, he came out from under the bed, picked up both of them, placed them on his shoulders, and took to the houses of his relatives shouting, "My wife is no unfaithful wench, as you claim she is. She is a chaste wife who has broken the vow of marital fidelity only to protect me from death."

Panchatantra

Another collection of tales was put together to inform the reader about the nature of clever adulteresses:

A merchant had to go on a voyage, leaving his young and beautiful wife all alone for sixty-nine nights. Fearing that his wife might be unfaithful while he was away, the merchant told his pet birds, a female mynah and a male parrot, to keep an eye on her and stop her from doing the undesirable. On the first night itself, as the wife prepared to visit her paramour, the mynah gave her a moral sermon. Irritated, the wife wrenched off the mynah bird's neck. Then the wise old parrot asked the wife if she knew the tricks of getting out of compromising situations familiar to all accomplished adulteresses. The wife did not and begged the parrot to enlighten her. Every night, just as the wife was about to leave the house, the parrot would tell the story of one clever adulteress, stretching it through the night, riveting the woman with the plot until daybreak. In this way he told her sixty-nine stories and kept her virtue intact for sixty-nine nights. Having heard all these tales, the wife realized that being an adulteress required skills she did not possess. She decided against visiting her lover. Luckily, that very night her husband returned, and the two made love within the confines of marital laws.

Sukasaptati

It is said that many men became monks out of disgust with the sexual appetite of adulterous women:

A sage gave King Bhratrihari the sweetest mango in the world. Bhratihari did not eat, preferring to gift it to the woman he loved most—his wife. The queen gave it to the stable boy with whom she was having an affair. The stable boy presented it to a peasant girl who had won his heart. The peasant girl felt she was unworthy of such a fruit, so she presented it to King Bhratrihari, who thus became aware of the faithlessness of his wife. Disgusted, he renounced his throne and became a monk.

Vetalapanchavinsati

Stories such as this fueled paranoia about a woman's virtue. It became necessary to find ways and means to restrain the nymph's sexuality.

Dangerous Damsels

Like her sexuality, a woman's beauty was a threat to social order. It could arouse unbridled desire, and the resulting kama could make man turn away from dharma. In ancient Hindu society beauty was considered a dangerous stimulant to primal, undisciplined urges. All women who were aware of their beauty were considered crafty, threats to social order:

Dashratha, king of Ayodhya, had three wives. His second wife, Kaikeyi, was his favorite; she was beautiful, intelligent, and brave. She would go hunting with her husband and even join him in battle. Once, in the thick of battle, as Dasharatha's chariot was being quickly maneuvered across enemy lines, the bolt of the chariot wheel fell out. When Kaikeyi noticed that the wheel was about to slip out, she inserted her thumb in the bolt hole, keeping the wheel in place and the chariot steady. On learning of Kaikeyi's bravery, Dasharatha offered her two boons. "I will reserve them for the future." Years later Dasharatha decided to renounce the world and pass on his crown to Rama, his eldest son by his eldest queen, Kaushalya. To secure the throne for her son, Kaikeyi made use of the two boons given to her by her husband long ago. "I want you to crown my son Bharata king and order Rama to go to the forest and live as a hermit for four-

teen years." Dasharatha, bound by his word and unable to deny anything to his beautiful wife, was forced to comply. He bitterly regretted losing his heart to this beautiful woman with a wicked heart.

Ramayana, Brahma Purana

Royal counselors prevented kings from marrying extremely beautiful women, fearing that their charms could distract the king from his royal duties:

A merchant wanted the king Yashodhana to marry his daughter Unmadini. The king's counselors were dispatched to inspect and appraise the prospective bride. Astounded by her amazing beauty, the counselors feared that she would corrupt the king and distract him from his dharma. Accordingly, they returned and informed the king that she was very ugly. Rather than reject the proposal, the king ordered the merchant to give his daughter to the commander of his armies. Unmadini never forgave the king for rejecting her and waited for an opportunity to avenge her humiliation. During a spring festival, as the king moved through the streets on his elephant, Unmadini stood naked on the terrace of her house and showed herself to the king. Infatuated by her beauty, Yashodhana sent his spies to learn more about her. When he learned that she was the merchant's daughter, he flew into a fit of rage and banished his counselors from his kingdom. Learning of the king's desire for his wife, the commander offered to send his wife to him, but because that is against dharma, Yashodhana refused the offer. The commander even offered to divorce his wife and turn her into a courtesan, thus making

her accessible to all, including the king, without breaking social law. But the king refused.
Unable to control his passion, realizing the
malignant effect of kama, the king renounced
his crown and became a hermit.

Katha-sarit-sagar

When a woman was extremely beautiful,
it was taken for granted that she could not be
faithful. In ancient India such women were
ordered to become courtesans and serve as
public wives. Unfaithful women caught by
husbands and rejected by society also sought
refuge in brothels. They were not treated with
dishonor. They were seen as safety valves for
the unbridled sexual urges of men, which could
otherwise subvert social order. The courtesans
were renowned for their capriciousness:

✳

Vikramsingh, king of Pratisthana, was
driven out of his city by intruders. He disguised himself and took refuge in the house
of the courtesan Kumudika in the city of
Ujjain. The courtesan served the king with
love and devotion. The king was impressed
by her service, but the king's companions
warned him to be wary of a beautiful
woman's affections. To test Kumudika, the
king feigned death. His companions carried
him to the crematorium. As they were about
to light the funeral pyre, Kumudika expressed her desire to die with the king, for
she loved him like a husband. Her decision
convinced Vikramsingh that her love for him
was genuine. When he revealed his true identity, Kumudika offered all her wealth to enable Vikramsingh to raise an army and win
his kingdom back. "Why are you doing this?"
asked the king. "In the hope that you also
attack and conquer Ujjain and save my lover

who is locked up in the prison," replied the
courtesan with a sly smile. The king realized that it was impossible to gauge a
courtesan's heart.

Katha-sarit-sagar

For the sake of social order, a woman's sexuality had to be fettered to her husband, her
beauty revealed only during the fertile period.
For the rest of the time, she had to be locked
away in the inner quarters of the household,
unseen even by the husband.

Restraining the Nymph

The fear of being cuckolded haunted men
most. In the following story found from the
Thai version of the Ramayana, a man's worst
nightmare comes true:

Ahalya had sexual relations with the sun-
god and the rain-god while her husband, the
sage Gautama, was away. She bore each
god a son and passed them off as the sons of
Gautama. Anjani, Ahalya's daughter by
Gautama, however, told her father how he
was being cuckolded. Enraged, Gautama
drove his "sons" out of his hermitage and
cursed them to turn into monkeys. Ahalya
cursed Anjani that she, too, would give birth
to a monkey. Anjani was standing atop a
mountain worshipping Shiva when the wind-
god Vayu made love to her. From that union
was born the monkey-god Hanuman.

Ramakien

Variants of how Ahalya cuckolded
Gautama are found in many Indian folk sto-

ries. A more popular story, however, is how Gautama punished Ahalya for having sex outside marriage:

When the sage Gautama discovered Indra, king of the gods, in bed with his wife, Ahalya, he castrated Indra and cursed his wife to turn into a stone that would be stepped on by all creatures. Years later, Rama—the noble prince of Ayodhya—placed his foot on this stone and, with the purity of his being, washed away Ahalya's sin.

Ramayana

One sage beheaded his wife simply because she had adulterous thoughts:

Renuka, wife of sage Jamadagni, was so chaste that she could collect water in unbaked pots. But one day she saw a handsome king sporting with his wives in the river. She had adulterous thoughts that caused her to lose her unique power. Enraged, her husband ordered his son Parashurama to behead his mother.

Folklore from the
state of Karnataka

To bridle a woman's sexual instincts, the carrot-and-stick approach was used. In the above story, the stick was social ignominy and brutal punishment. The carrot was magical powers that stem from chastity. Renuka's ability to collect water in unbaked pots comes from *sat*, the power of chastity, the product of a totally domesticated womb that sustains society. When a woman is true to her husband in body, mind, and soul, she acquires sat and transforms into a *sati*.

Powers of Wifely Virtue

The word *sati* evokes great awe and respect among Hindus. A chaste woman is considered as holy as a celibate man. She is the foundation of human society, a being who has triumphed over primal urges and thus is worthy of adoration:

Shiva's nakedness aroused the wives of forest hermits. When the forest hermits discovered this, they attacked Shiva with sticks and stones. Bruised and battered, Shiva sought shelter in Vasistha's house. Vasistha was away but his wife took him in and nursed him back to health. She looked upon his naked body, which had aroused so many women, with maternal affection. Pleased with her chastity, Shiva blessed Arundhati.

Shiva Purana

A chaste woman's sat, like a chaste man's tapas, is acquired by bridling natural urges with mental discipline. Just as nymphs test the celibacy of a rishi, the gods test the chastity of a sati:

The beautiful princess Sukanya, daughter of King Saryati, pushed a twig into a termite hill unaware that within the hill sat an old hermit called Chyavana. The twig blinded Chyavana and destroyed his tapas. He threatened Saryati with a curse. To make amends, the king gave his daughter's hand in marriage to the old blind sage. One day the twin gods, the Ashwini, known for their beauty and virility, approached Sukanya and asked her to abandon her old husband and make love to them. She rejected their offer and remained true to her husband. The gods then took Chyavana to a pond where all three took a dip and emerged looking equally attractive. Sukanya, in her chastity, recognized and chose her husband. The Ashwini blessed the chaste Sukanya so that she could make love and enjoy conjugal bliss with the rejuvenated Chyavana.

Shatapatha Brahmana, Jaiminiya Brahmana, Mahabharata, Devi Bhagvatam

In another story the sati penalizes those who dare test her virtue:

Brahma, Vishnu, and Shiva decided to test the chastity of Anasuya, wife of the sage Atri. They went to her house disguised as young brahmanas and said, "We have been fasting for a month and have sworn not to break our fast until a woman lets us suckle milk from her breasts." Compelled by the laws of hospitality, Anasuya agreed to let the handsome youths suckle her breasts. But as she undid her bodice, such was the power of her chastity that the three gods turned into three babies and Anasuya was able to nurse them without loss of her wifely virtue. Impressed by her purity, the gods declared that she would bear a son called Dattatreya who would contain within him the spirits of Brahma, Vishnu, and Shiva.

Folklore from the state of Maharashtra

Both sat and tapas are used to manipulate the forces of the cosmos in one's favor. A woman's restrained fertility is good for worldly life, just as a man's retrained virility is good for spiritual life. Sacred Hindu lore is filled with tales of a chaste woman's magical powers:

Gandhari was so chaste that when she learned that the man she was to marry was blind, she blindfolded herself so that she could share her husband's misfortune. As she bottled up the power of her eyes, her gaze acquired tremendous powers. She decided to use it to save her wicked son, Duryodhana. Before he rode out to battle, she asked him to appear before her naked. "By the power of my gaze, I will make your skin so powerful that no weapon will penetrate it," she said. When Duryodhana was about to enter his mother's room naked, Krishna appeared on the scene and told him that as a grown man he had to have enough shame to cover his genitals and thighs when he appeared before his mother. Duryodhana covered his genitals with a few leaves and stood before his mother. She removed her blindfold for the first time in her life and looked upon her son. When she discovered that his underparts were covered, she wept and covered her eyes once again. "Foolish boy, there is a chink in the armor my chastity bestowed upon you," cried Gandhari. True enough, in the battle at Kurukshetra Duryodhana could not be harmed by any weapon until Bhima's mace smashed his thighs and crushed his genitals.

Folklore based on Mahabharata from the state of Haryana

With the power of chastity, a sati could protect herself from all harm. In the following story, the chaste wife uses sat to destroy the man who tries to rape her:

Damayanti's husband Nala gambled away his kingdom in a game of dice. Destitute, he was

*forced to leave his city and seek shelter in the
forest. As befitting a dutiful wife, Damayanti
decided to share her husband's misfortune and follow him into the forest. While in the forest, Nala
could not bear to see his wife suffer for his mis-
deeds. He ran away, hoping that she would go
back to her father's house and live in comfort.
Abandoned by her husband, Damayanti lost
her way in the forest. She was caught by a
python and would have died had a hunter not
come to her rescue. Finding her all alone, the
hunter decided to have his way with her. When
he tried to touch her, he burst into flames. Such
was the power of Damayanti's chastity.*

Mahabharata

Such tales led to the belief that if a woman
was raped, it was because she did not have
adequate sat to protect her—she was not
chaste enough. A victim of rape was thus held
responsible for her crime.

Testing Fidelity with Fire

When aspersions were cast on a woman's character, the onus of demonstrating sat and con-
firming her chastity fell upon the woman. For
this, she had to go through a trial by fire.

The fire-god Agni's capacity to burn was
believed to be a manifestation of his unquenchable erotic desire. No woman was safe
from his fiery passion. He could, however,
never cast his lustful gaze on chaste wives.
Their sat protected them from being singed
by the flames of his desire:

*The fire-god Agni fell in love with the wives
of the seven celestial sages and decided to*

*make love to them with heat and light every
time they came near him. He thus successfully managed to make love to six sage wives
and make them pregnant. However, no
matter how hard he tried, he could not make
love to Arundhati, wife of Vasistha. Such
was her chastity.*

Mahabharata, Skanda Purana

Many patriarchs concluded that the best
way to test a woman's fidelity was to make
her go through a trial by fire, or *agni-pariksha*.
If fire did not harm her, it meant she possessed sat by remaining true to her husband.
The most famous trial by fire in sacred Hindu
lore is that of Sita, the embodiment of wifely
virtue:

*After rescuing his wife, Sita, from the clutches
of the rakshasa-king Ravana, Rama asked
her to go through a trial by fire to show the
world that she had been faithful to him even
though she had lived under another man's
roof. Sita sat on a pile of wood and ordered
her brother-in-law Laxmana to light the fire.
The flames did not even singe her hair. The
fire-god Agni himself appeared and testified
to Sita's good character. Pleased with this,
Rama accepted Sita as his wife.*

Ramayana, Skanda Purana

However, the trial by fire was not fool-
proof—as one learns from the following story:

*A brahmana discovered that his wife was
unfaithful to him. When she pleaded her innocence, he ordered her to undergo a trial
by fire to prove her chastity. When the adul-*

Sita's chastity being tested by fire. Chitrakathi painting; Paithan, Maharashtra. Nineteenth century.

terous wife stepped into the pit of fire, the flames did not harm her. Surprised, the brahmana demanded an explanation from the fire-god Agni. Agni explained that the place where his wife had liaisons with other men was a holy spot where all sins are washed away. Hence, though adulterous, she was still chaste.

Skanda Purana

Perhaps that is the reason why the people of Ayodhya doubted Sita's fidelity when she returned to Ayodhya:

Rama returned to Ayodhya after spending fourteen years in the forest and was imme-diately crowned king by his people. They all had heard how his wife, Sita, had been abducted by the rakshasa-king Ravana and how Rama had rescued her from the island kingdom of Lanka. Everyone wondered whether Sita had remained faithful to Rama. One day the queen mother Kaikeyi, Rama's step-mother, who had been responsible for his exile in the first place, asked Sita to draw her an image of Ravana. "I never looked at him. I only once glanced at his shadow as he was carrying me across the sea." Coaxed by Kaikeyi, Sita drew the outline of Ravana's shadow. When she left the room, Kaikeyi completed the picture and then showed it to Rama, planting seeds of suspicion in his heart.

Folklore based on the Ramayana

Eventually, the people of Ayodhya refuse to accept Sita as their queen, and Rama is forced to take cognizance of their wishes:

Not long after his coronation, Rama's spies informed him that people were speaking ill of his wife. They did not appreciate his accepting Sita as his wife after she had spent time in the house of Ravana, a rakshasa known for his virility and power over women. When Rama learned this, he was heartbroken. He loved Sita but did not want to smear his family's good name. So he ordered Sita to leave his palace and his city and live in the forest.

Uttara Ramayana

Sita's exile from Ayodhya is a contentious issue in sacred Hindu lore. Rama is considered the most virtuous man to walk on earth, an incarnation of the god Vishnu himself. Many wonder how he could abandon a wife who had proved her chastity. How could he succumb to popular pressure when he knew what was right? Endless debates have been raised on the subject. What is interesting is that although Rama abandons the woman his people do not want as queen, he refuses to marry another woman. Rama's fidelity to Sita is unique in sacred Hindu lore. Most Hindu gods and heroes have more than one wife. Only Rama has the unique distinction of being *ekam-patni-vrata*, "one who is eternally faithful to a single wife."

As king, Rama is obliged to perform many yagnas. Since no man can participate in this sacred ritual without a wife sitting beside him, he places an idol of Sita made out of gold on the seat reserved for his queen. That he uses the purest metal on earth to mold the image of Sita is noteworthy.

Later in the epic one is told how Sita gives birth to Rama's sons, a pair of twins, in the forest and how, years later, the boys find Rama's royal horse and refuse to part with it. A great battle ensues between the soldiers of Ayodhya and the two young boys. By the power of Sita's sat, the boys manage to defeat Rama's army. Still the people of Ayodhya refuse to accept Sita as queen. Then an event occurs that forces them to accept Sita's purity:

A thousand-headed rakshasa attacked Ayodhya, and it was said that only a chaste woman could kill him. Every woman in the city entered the battlefield but failed to harm the terrible rakshasa. Finally, the people of Ayodhya begged Rama to send for Sita. Sita entered the battle, picked up a bow, and shot an arrow straight through the rakshasa's heart, killing him instantly.

Devi Bhagvatam

Despite getting this proof of her chastity, the people of Ayodhya insist on another fire-test before accepting Sita as queen. Tired of having to prove her virtue repeatedly, Sita asks the earth to open and take her into its bowels if she is pure enough. Instantly, a great chasm appears, and from within rises a golden throne for Sita. As Sita disappears into the earth seated on the throne, flowers rain from the heavens—for Sita is no ordinary woman. Plowed out of earth by her father, King Janaka of Mithila, she is the earth-goddess Bhudevi herself.

After Sita's disappearance, Rama renounces worldly life, gives up his body by entering the River Sarayu, and returns as Vishnu to Vaikuntha, his abode in the sky, to look upon and take care of the earth-goddess forever.

All Hindus worship Sita as the embodiment of wifely virtue.

The Armor of Chastity

One of the most celebrated satis in Hindu lore is Savitri, who by her wit saved her husband from the jaws of death:

Savitri married the woodcutter Satyavan, although he was destined to die within a year of marriage. On that fateful day Savitri saw Yama, god of death, cast his noose and capture Satayavan's life breath. As he moved away on his buffalo, she decided to follow him to the land of the dead. Yama tried his best to give Savitri the slip, but no matter how hard he tried Savitri was determined to follow Yama to the land of the dead. "If you turn away I will give you anything but the life of your husband," he said. Savitri asked that she have a hundred sons by Satyavan. "So be it," said Yama and continued his journey. Some time later he found Savitri still following him. "Why are you still following me?" he asked. "I thought we had a deal." "Yes, we did," replied Savitri, "but how can I bear Satyavan a hundred sons when you are taking away his life breath?" Yama realized that Savitri had outsmarted him and tricked him into releasing Satyavan's life breath.

Mahabharata

The tale of Savitri is narrated each year to married Hindu women, who then tie a thread round a banyan tree, praying that their husbands live as long as the perennial tree. There is no Hindu ceremony or ritual in which a husband prays for the long life of his wife.

A Hindu wife is considered responsible for her husband's life, because the powers of chastity protect her husband from harm:

Ugrashrava was a wicked man, but his wife, Shilavati, served him dutifully. When he contracted leprosy, she begged on the streets to feed him. When he became lame, she carried him on her shoulders. When he had the urge to visit a prostitute, she took him there. The sage Mandavya was so disgusted by the sight of the lame leper Ugrashrava traveling to a prostitute's house on his chaste wife's shoulder that he decreed that Ugrashrava would die at sunrise. Shilavati then used the powers of her chastity to prevent the sun from rising. Anasuya, wife of Atri, finally persuaded Shilavati to let the sun rise and accept the inevitable death of her husband.

Brahmanda Purana

A woman's chastity generates an armor of invincibility around her husband. To destroy this armor, devas use their guile to make the wives of their eternal enemies, asuras, unchaste:

The gods could not kill the demon Shankhachuda because he was protected by the power of his wife's chastity. The only way to kill him, they realized, was to make his wife, Vrinda, lose her wifely virtue. So Vishnu, champion of the gods, took the form of Shankhachuda and visited Vrinda in her bedchamber while Shiva engaged the real Shankhachuda in the battlefield. Vrinda, unable to recognize the impostor, made love

to him and lost her purity. With that, Shankhachuda became vulnerable to the weapons of the gods and was killed by Shiva.

Padma Purana

Vrinda's chastity is compromised for the good of the world. The whole world holds her responsible for the death of her husband. Only Vishnu knows that she has been a true wife. He offers her shelter in his celestial abode, Vaikuntha. Vishnu's consort, the goddess Laxmi, however, refuses to share her house or her husband's affection with another woman. She does not let Vrinda enter the inner apart-ments. Helpless and destitute, Vrinda refuses to budge from Vishnu's courtyard. In time, her feet turn into roots and her arms sprout leaves. She turns into the fragrant tulsi plant. Vishnu, who cannot not come to her rescue, turns into a *shalagrama* stone.

Vaishnavas call the tulsi plant Vishnupriya, "beloved of Vishnu," because Vrinda's steadfast though unrequited devotion won her an eternal place in Vishnu's heart. Vishnu worship is incomplete without offerings of sprigs of this plant. Because Vishnu could not come to her rescue, she is brought to him. In deference to Laxmi, however, the plant is always kept in the court-

Worship of the tulsi plant in the courtyard of a Hindu household. Chitrakathi painting; Paithan, Maharashtra. Nineteenth century.

yard, never in the inner quarters of the house.

The tulsi plant is an integral part of the Hindu household. Chaste Hindu women are advised to nurture and worship the sacred basil plant in their houses. Every dawn, after a bath and before beginning household chores, married women of the household worship this plant. They pour water, wave lamps, and circumambulate the specially designed altar on which the plant is grown. The plant is a reminder of the importance of sat in keeping husbands alive and ushering happiness and prosperity into the household.

Burning Widows

Sat is the product of a totally domesticated womb. It forms the bedrock of a stable society. Belief in sat was and still is the most powerful means of ensuring a woman's fidelity in Hindu society. It mentally pressures a woman to be faithful under all circumstances. If she is chaste, her husband is alive, her children healthy, and her household prosperous. She is respected in society as an auspicious suhagan and invited to all wedding and birth ceremonies. If she is unchaste, her household collapses and her husband dies. She becomes an inauspicious widow, shunned by all.

When a man died before his wife, it meant that the woman did not have sufficient sat to protect her husband from death. The only option left for a woman to reaffirm her chastity was to burn herself on her husband's funeral pyre. She would bedeck herself in bright clothes, distribute her wealth among the poor, and sit on the pile of logs, placing her husband's head in her lap and then ordering the fire to be lit. Her sat apparently protected her from feeling the pain as flames singed her

clothes and burnt her flesh. She then transformed into Sati Maharani, the personification of chastity, the embodiment of wifely virtue, a goddess to be adored by all women:

The Pandavas defeated the Kauravas and emerged victorious in the Kurukshetra war. Gandhari, the mother of the Kauravas, was furious to learn that they had not spared even one of her sons. Because Krishna had successfully maneuvered the Pandavas to victory, Gandhari held him responsible for the death of all her sons. She cursed Krishna that he would die like a common beast. So it

Palmprints of women who immolated themselves following the death of their warrior husbands, and thus came to be identified as Rani-Sati. Jodhpur fort, Rajasthan. Eighteenth century.

came to pass that, years after the war, while Krishna was resting in the forest under a tree, a hunter shot a poisoned dart mistaking his foot as the ear of a deer. When Krishna was cremated, four of his wives, including Rukmini and Jambhavati, joined him on the funeral pyre. The remaining four wives, including Satyabhama and Kalindi, went to the forest to lead ascetic lives.

Mahabharata

The word *sati* is linked to Shiva's first wife, who killed herself to destroy a ceremony that sought to insult her husband:

Sati was the daughter of Daksha, the primal patriarch of samaja. She chose Shiva as her husband and unconditionally accepted his maverick lifestyle, his lack of guile, his lack of pretence, and his refusal to follow social conventions. Daksha did not appreciate Shiva's ways and became particularly hostile after the ascetic god refused to salute him. To insult Shiva, Daksha conducted a grand yagna and invited everyone except Shiva. Sati considered this an oversight and went to the yagna, though Shiva refused to accompany her. There she learned the truth. Her father insulted her husband and no one stopped him. "I would rather die than hear such things about my beloved," said Sati. She decided to kill herself by jumping into the fire altar. The fire-god Agni could not burn her. She had too much sat in her. So Sati created her own fire by the power of sat and incinerated herself.

Shiva Purana, Vishnu Purana

A good wife is supposed to make sure that her husband's reputation is never soiled, even after death. It was considered better to die than risk the world berating the dead husband for being unable to protect his wife from rapists. All these ideas were used to justify burning a widow:

A civil war led to the death of all the Yadava men, and Dwarka became a city of widows. The Pandava Arjuna offered the destitute women shelter in his city. As he led them through the forest, they were attacked by forest tribes that abducted and raped the women. Some of the women managed to escape and drowned themselves in the River Sarasvati. Their souls went straight to heaven.

Mahabharata

In medieval times widows of warriors would voluntarily burn themselves rather than face the humiliation of rape. This was *jowhar*, an act of self-destruction to uphold the honor of the husband, the destruction of the field before another farmer could claim it.

A truly chaste wife, a *pativrata*, it was said, did not have to burn herself on her husband's funeral pyre. She died the moment her husband breathed his last:

To test the love of Padmavati for her husband, the poet Jayadeva, the queen of Kalinga told her that her husband had been killed while accompanying the king on a hunt. Instantly, Padmavati collapsed on the floor and her heart stopped beating. In panic, the queen sent for the king and the poet. The poet simply touched his virtuous wife with love, and she opened her eyes as if from a slumber.

Bhakti-mala

A pativrata had firm faith that she would not be alive if her husband were dead:

Ravana used his magic powers to conjure the head of Rama. He had it sent to Sita on a tray. "Now that your husband is dead, the law of marital fidelity no longer applies to you," said the rakshasa-king. "Your sorcery will not fool me," said Sita with conviction, "for if he were dead, I would have been dead, too." The confidence of the virtuous wife destroyed Ravana's apparition, and the truth behind the severed head was revealed.

Ramayana

It is said that a true wife walks beside her husband through seven lifetimes. She lives for him. If she dies before he does, all women worship her corpse, which is bedecked as a bride before being cremated. She is deified as *sada suhagan*, the eternally unwidowed matriarch.

Untainted Brides

The belief that a woman must be faithful to only one man over several lifetimes meant that a girl had to be chaste before and after marriage. Her virginity became a precious commodity. Fathers took great pains to secure their daughter's reputation:

For one year Arjuna had to disguise himself as a palace eunuch named Brihanalla and live in the women's quarters of Virata's palace. He taught dance to the king's daughter Uttara. At the end of the year, when Arjuna revealed his identity, the king feared that no man would want to marry Uttara, because she had shared her quarters with a man. To comfort the king, Arjuna declared that as her dance teacher he considered Uttara his child and accepted her as his daughter-in-law. Uttara married Arjuna's son Abhimanyu.

Mahabharata

In the following story a princess cannot get married because a man touched her body before her marriage. She therefore spends the rest of her life with her girlfriend. Some scholars have commented on the suggestions of lesbianism in this narrative:

Ratnavali, daughter of the king of Anarta, and Brahmini, daughter of the priest of Anarta, were the best of friends. They could not bear the thought of being separated after marriage. They preferred death. On learning of the intensity of their emotion, the king decided that the two girls would be given in marriage to the same household—Ratnavali would marry the king, and Brahmani would marry the resident priest. It so happened that a brahmana youth in Anarta had visited a prostitute and consumed wine. To wash away the sin, he had the choice of drinking scalding-hot butter or touching the breasts of a virgin princess, considering her to be his mother. The youth's parents begged the king of Anarta to let their son touch his daughter, because the other recommended method for expiation of sin was lethal. The king relented, and the brahmana youth touched Ratnavali's breasts thinking of her as his mother. Ratnavali was told to look upon the

youth as her son. Instantly, her breasts oozed milk. When the news spread, no man wanted to marry Ratnavali, as she had been tainted. Brahmani, too, could not marry, because she waited for sixteen years for Ratnavali to marry and was therefore too old to be a bride. The two unmarried girls left their parent's house, sought refuge in the forest, and performed penance. Shiva appeared before Brahmani and blessed her. Brahmani refused to take the blessing until Shiva appeared before Ratnavali and blessed her, too. The place where Shiva blessed the two girls became a holy place.

Skanda Purana

Shaved Heads and White Saris

Samaja fetters a woman's fertility to one man. In Hindu society, when the husband dies, the wife is not allowed to remarry. She can kill herself on his funeral pyre. If she does not, there is the problem of her unrestrained sexual instinct:

After the death of her husband, Mahi left her son Sanajjata in the hermitage of sage Galava and went to live a free life. Years later Sanajjata ran away from the hermitage and went to a place called Janasthana where he had sexual relations with a woman, not realizing she was none other than Mahi. For unknowingly having sexual relations with his mother, Sanajjata contracted leprosy. When Galava divined what had happened, he ordered mother and son to bathe in a holy lake and wash their sins away.

Brahma Purana

Without a farmer to tend the field, the field turns into a forest. Without a husband who demands chastity, a widow can become a prostitute and bring dishonor to her husband's memory:

A young widow took her husband's ashes to Mathura, where she was seen by prostitutes who indoctrinated her in the ways of a harlot. Years later a young man visited her brothel and, after having sexual relations with her, contracted a dreadful disease. The sage Sumanta divined that the prostitute whom the young man had visited was his elder sister, widowed long ago. When the prostitute learned of this, she killed herself in shame. The brother was advised to go on a pilgrimage and wash away his sin by bathing in holy waters.

Varaha Purana

A good widow is expected to remain chaste to her husband's memory:

Bhattika was a child widow. Her husband had died before she had attained puberty. Condemned to eternal virginity, Bhattika dedicated her life to god and spent her time singing songs to the glory of Shiva. The serpent-king Vasuki and his friend Takshaka heard her sing and fell in love with her. They abducted her and carried her off to the subterranean city of nagas known as Bhogavati. "Marry both of us. Human laws do not apply here," said Takshaka. Bhattika refused and cursed Takshaka that he would lose his immortal serpent form and become a mortal man. Takshaka begged for mercy. Bhattika

relented and said the curse would not come true if he took her back to earth. When Bhattika returned, no one in her village believed she was still chaste. To demonstrate her purity, she took the fire-test. She was so pure that fire turned to water.

Skanda Purana

In the Padma Purana a widow forced to remain faithful to her dead husband censures her vagina: "Why do you itch, my yoni? It is sinful that another man enters you." When the itch does not stop, she inserts her finger to please her vagina and finally embraces the foot of her bedstead and presses her breasts against it.

A good Hindu widow, like a good Hindu wife, does not look at any other man. Without her husband, her fertility has no use. So she suppresses it, systemically and cosmetically. Not wanting to attract amorous attentions or arouse uncontrolled passion, she shaves her beautiful hair, wears drab white garments, and leaves her body unadorned. She smothers her sexual desires. As she suffers, she prays for a better life with her husband in her next birth.

Even in death a husband restrains the widow's primal urge, which can subvert the edifice of civilization built on female chastity.

The widower, however, is free to remarry.

CHAPTER FIVE

Goddesses with Unbound Hair

RECLAIMING THE CIRCLE

Nature's Unwholesome Side

The walls of civilization cannot shut out the dark side of samsara. Nature shrugs and there is flood, famine, and fire. Adulterous desires emerge across caste lines. Women miscarry. Children die. Social order is disrupted when the goddess bares her fangs, unbinds her hair, and dances naked, unmindful of disapproving stares. Suddenly, samaja is forced to contend with the emotions that dharma tries so hard to contain.

Samsara is not just beautiful. It is also horrible. Beyond every green meadow, under every flowering tree, is a dark chthonian secret—a rotting corpse, a simmering volcano. Life and death, creation and destruction, sex and violence coexist in Nature. When the gods and demons churned the ocean of milk, the nectar of immortality—amrita—did not rise alone. With it came a deadly poison called *kalakuta*:

⁂

As the sons of Prajapati churned the milky waters of the ocean of life, there emerged from the depths of the waters a viscid and caustic fluid, frothing with fury, polluting the air with deadly fumes. Terrified, the sons of Prajapati turned to their father, who summoned Shiva. The hermit-god collected the poison and drank it as if it were sweet wine.

Shiva Purana

If amrita represents the radiant and fertile side of samsara, then kalakuta represents its dark and barren side. Shiva could consume kalakuta because he is lord of yoga. Yoga gives him the mental discipline to face the brutality of Nature. Shiva is the only Hindu god whose divinity is seen in the light of funeral pyres. He can withstand the stench of death. That is one of the reasons the goddess chose him as her consort:

Devi created Brahma, Vishnu, and Shiva. She decided to divide herself into three parts and give herself to the gods. First, she decided to test them. She took the form of a worm-infested corpse. Disgusted by her appearance, Brahma turned, while Vishnu plunged into the waters. Only Shiva embraced the corpse without fear or loathing. Pleased, the goddess married him in her totality. As Sarasvati, her intellectual side, she married Brahma. As Laxmi, her bountiful side, she married Vishnu.

Mahabhagvata Purana,
Brihaddharma Purana

Shiva swallowed kalakuta but did not destroy it. As he was about to swallow the lethal drink, his consort Parvati grabbed his neck and choked him until the kalakuta remained in his neck, turning it blue. Why did the goddess stop Shiva and turn him into the blue-throated god? Shiva could have easily digested the poison. However, had he done so, amrita would not have emerged. The dark side of Nature balances the bright side of Nature. They are two aspects of the same goddess:

Brahma had decreed that demon Daruka would not die at the hands of a man, beast, or god. This left him vulnerable only to attacks by women. The devas, tormented by Daruka, sought the aid of the goddess Parvati, who immersed herself in the poison locked in Shiva's throat and transformed into Kali, the dark one. When she returned to Mount Kailas after killing the demon, her skin was black, her eyes red, her teeth like fangs, her tongue blood smeared. She hardly looked like a wife. Shiva laughed. Hurt, the goddess performed austerities, bathed in a river, and transformed into Gauri, the bright one. Her golden skin, shapely eyes, pearl-like teeth, and smile aroused Shiva. He embraced her and they made love.

Shiva Purana, Linga Purana

Mistress of Misfortune

The cosmic ascetic understands and transcends the dark and the bright sides of Nature. Hence, Shiva's consort Parvati has a dual personality: She is both mother and killer, Gauri and Kali. Images of Gauri show her dressed in bright clothes, bedecked with flowers and jewels, and holding a cane of sugar, a parrot, a lotus, and a mirror in her four hands. Sugarcane is the love-god Kama's bow; the parrot, his mount. The lotus represents the female generative organ. The mirror reflects

A nymph adorning herself as she celebrates life (left); a yogini holding a skull-mace as she confronts death. Thus the female form embodies the principles of both generation and destruction. Stone carvings from the queen's stepwell of Patan, Gujarat. Eleventh century.

beauty. The goddess clearly personifies Nature's life-giving and love-arousing capability. Kali, on the other hand, personifies Nature's life-taking and fear-generating capacity. Her images show her naked, covered with severed limbs and human entrails, holding a sword, a human head, and a bowl filled with blood.

Vishnu's consort Laxmi, unlike Shiva's, radiates only the good things of samsara—beauty, bounty, and benevolence. As the keeper of order and sustainer of civilization, Vishnu cannot embrace the unwholesome side of Nature. While samaja welcomes Laxmi, goddess of fortune, it shuts the door to Alaxmi, goddess of misfortune, the very embodiment of kalakuta, who also emerged from the ocean of milk.

Alaxmi is everything Laxmi is not—gaunt, ugly, foul smelling, with sharp teeth, barren womb, and shriveled breasts. She dwells wherever there is dirt, darkness, and ugliness. Every evening the Hindu housewife cleans the house, decorates the threshold with sacred symbols, lights a lamp, opens the front door, and beckons Laxmi into the house. The garbage is dumped outside and the back door locked to prevent Alaxmi from slipping in and stealing the family happiness:

Alaxmi and Laxmi visited a merchant and asked him, "Which of us, in your opinion, is more beautiful?" The merchant was in a fix; he knew the penalty for angering either goddess. So he said, "I think Laxmi is beautiful when she enters my house and Alaxmi is beautiful when she leaves my house." On hearing this, Laxmi rushed into the merchant's house, while Alaxmi ran out. As a result the merchant's business boomed,

profits soared, money poured in, and with it came power, prestige, and position.

Folklore from the state of Orissa

In sacred Hindu scriptures Alaxmi is described as Laxmi's elder sister. Her divine status is always acknowledged, but her presence is never desired. She is that part of Nature nobody wants within the house. She lurks outside happy and prosperous homes waiting for an opportunity to step in. Opportunity arrives when there are quarrels, or when there is sloth, dirt, and indiscipline.

Ceremonies invoking the powers of the goddess acknowledge both her manifestations. Some rituals draw in her benevolent grace. Others shut out her malevolent gaze. The antiseptic turmeric repels barrenness, while vermilion attracts fertility. Sweetmeats entice Laxmi. Sour, pungent, and astringent food satisfies and keeps away Alaxmi. Storekeepers in the western state of Maharashtra place an image of Laxmi near the cash register; before it they light a lamp and make offerings of flowers, incense, and sweets. They also tie a lemon and green chilies outside their shops, keeping Alaxmi in mind. When the mistress of misfortune arrives, she eats her favorite foods to her heart's content and turns around without bothering to step in. When women worship Santoshi, the goddess of satisfaction, they never eat sour food. They eat only sweets. Sweetness invokes the goddess of joy, sourness, the goddess of suffering.

The Ultimate Calamity

Death is the ultimate misfortune. No ritual can keep it out. Death to the Hindu is a goddess who came from the very source that brought forth life:

When Brahma created all creatures of the world, they multiplied themselves until the universe was overcrowded with living beings. This made Brahma angry. He scowled, and out of his scowl came Mrityu, the goddess of death, dressed in red. The goddess wept when she was told why she was created. Her tears became diseases. She did not like her task, but Brahma convinced her that her actions were necessary to rotate the wheel of life. "When you strike, there will be desire and anger in the heart of the dying man that will ensure his rebirth," said Brahma.

Mahabharata

Hindus also have a god of death called Yama:

The sun-god Surya married Saranya, the daughter of Tvastr, the celestial artisan. She gave birth to a pair of twins, Yama and Yami. Unable to withstand her husband's radiance, Saranya ran away, leaving behind her shadow, Chaya, to look after the twins. Surya could not distinguish between Saranya and Chaya and so did not notice his wife's absence. He fathered three children on Chaya. One of them was Manu, who went on to father the human race. Chaya mistreated her twin stepchildren. Unable to bear her cruelty, Yama kicked her. For this act, his leg became infested with maggots, and he was doomed to become the lord of the dead. When Surya learned what had transpired between Chaya and Yama, he concluded that Chaya was not his real wife. He went to his father-in-law's house in search of Saranya and learned the cause of her grief.

Tvastr chiseled away a portion of Surya's radiance and made his glare tolerable. Surya then set out in search of his wife. He found her grazing on earth in the form of a mare. Taking the form of a stallion, he made love to Saranya and she bore him twin sons, the Ashwinis, gods of potency.

Rig Veda, Mahabharata,
Matsya Purana

Surya's two wives—the gentle Saranyu and the harsh Chaya—give birth to Yama, lord of the dead, and Manu, lord of the living. The idea that life and death, fortune and misfortune, creation and destruction are twin aspects of the same material reality is consistent in Hinduism.

The personalities of the god and goddess of death are quite different. Yama's approach to death is logical, Mrityu's is more emotional. Yama arrives at the end of a lifetime; Mrityu can strike anytime.

Yama keeps a record of all human deeds and makes all creatures repay the debt of karma. He decides under what circumstances a creature should be born, taking into account deeds done in the past life. He thus maintains order in the cosmos and is considered a manifestation of dharma. There are no temples dedicated to Yama. Rituals neither please nor displease him. He is passionless. Nothing invites him or keeps him away. He kills when it is time to kill.

Only the goddess, as the following tale suggests, can bypass the law of Yama:

A woman brought her dead son to the goddess Karni and begged her to retore him to life. Karni approached Yama but he refused to help. Furious, the goddess decreed that her devotees would not be bound by Yama's

laws. So it is that Karni's devotees are re-
born as mice in her temple. When the mice
die they are reborn as her devotees.

Temple lore from the
state of Rajasthan

Mrityu, unlike Yama, is a divine shrew who kills when she is angry. She can kill a baby as soon as it leaves its mother's womb. She can kill a groom on his wedding night. She can overturn the decree of fate. She must be appeased and kept away. Her abode, the cremation ground, is located outside the village and considered inauspicious. Men who enter the cremation ground bathe and undergo ritual purification before they reenter their houses. Food for the goddess of death is always kept on the village frontier lest she wander into the village to satisfy her hunger.

The Wilderness Beyond

With death looming on the horizon, man seeks permanence in his life. When that is unavailable, he seeks some kind of certainty or predictability. He searches for patterns in the random flux of material reality. He establishes society, creates rules, and attempts to generate order. But beyond the square of civilization lurks an unfathomable realm of uncontrollable, incalculable, chaotic energy with the capacity to create and destroy life. Through prayers and incantations, the creative energy is harnessed and the destructive energy kept away.

Occasionally, the dark side does make its presence felt with unbelievable ferocity:

A merchant's ship was lost at sea and came

upon a fabulous island where he saw a great goddess under a great tree, surrounded by children and women, serpents and reptiles, cows and tigers. In her presence, the cat and mouse were at play and the wolf and the sheep were friends, as were the lion and the doe. The goddess herself was swallowing and disgorging herds of elephants. The goddess identified herself as Shitala and told the merchant that she would restore his ship to the port if he promised to institute her worship in his land. The merchant agreed and, on reaching his city, went immediately to his king and told him of his encounter with Shitala. The king did not believe the merchant and refused to worship the goddess. Enraged, Shitala struck the king's city with her army of diseases. Every man suffered from leprosy, every woman with cholera, every child with pox. Even the king was afflicted. He began worshipping the goddess, and instantly the diseases disappeared and the health of his subjects was restored.

Shitala Mangal

The dark side of Nature also lurks in the mind of man. Dharma restrains it. But occasionally it erupts. There is fear and fury. Uncontrollable rage is satisfied only with violence. Murders, riots, rape, and plunder follow. In the din of battle Korravai cackles, mocking pathetic human attempts to suppress the animal in man. Korravai is the goddess of battlefields, and is revered in southern India. And when the warriors depart, she feasts on the entrails of the dead along with dogs, vultures, and carrion crows. Those who wish to cremate dead warriors appease her before claiming the corpses:

Potaraju, the minion of the goddess of the

battlefields, complained why he and his horde of ghosts had to watch over dead bodies. "If I take care of a city or village instead, I will get food to it." The goddess assured him that the local communities would always feed him with a sheep as tall as a palm tree and with a mound of rice as high as a mountain for as long as they had rice and salt. The goddess then grew so tall that her head reached the sky. She projected twelve spears out of her head and impaled an elephant on each spear. Over each elephant, she stacked twelve corpses. On each corpse, she placed twelve lamps. In her twelve arms, she carried twelve dreadful blood-soaked weapons. With burning coals on her head and jingling bells on her feet, she presented herself to those who came to the battlefield to claim the bodies of fallen warriors. She yelled like thunder, set the skies aflame, and made sparks of fire fall on earth. Everyone trembled and saluted her. They offered her gifts. Pleased with the offerings, she disappeared, threatening to return if her minion, Potaraju, was not well fed and if she was not respected.

Folklore from the state
of Andhra Pradesh

Death, disease, and violence—manifesting as Mrityu, Shitala, and Korravai—humble the man who boasts of the grandeur of civilization. They are reminders that beyond that square of civilization, untamed by the laws of man, unexplained by logic, there exists a primal power that can overwhelm society anytime.

Wrath of the Child Savior

No law, no doctrine, no morals, no ethics, no barriers or boundaries can keep disease out of society. Rationality and repression come to naught when a little baby, red with rash and puckered with pox, burns with fever. Duty and detachment are waylaid as the primal urge for survival takes over. Unable to bear her child's delirious cry, the Hindu mother rushes to the shrine of Jari-Mari, the fiery goddess of fever, with gifts of bridal finery—vermilion and turmeric powder, bangles, flowers, a red sari, and some sweets. She sings songs to appease her wrath. She begs the goddess to turn into Shitala, the cool goddess of health.

The folk tradition of Hinduism recognizes innumerable malevolent female spirits who harm children. Even Krishna, the greatest of Vishnu's earthly incarnations, had to face one when he was a child:

When Kamsa learned that his newborn killer was being raised in secret, he ordered the wet nurse Putana to go round his kingdom and poison every newborn child with the venomous milk in her breasts. Putana did as she was told and soon mothers in surrounding villages were mourning over infant corpses. Putana finally came upon the baby Krishna in the house of Nanda in the village of cowherds. She slipped into the house when no one was around and began nursing the divine child. Her poisoned milk did not harm Krishna. Instead, he sucked out her life through her nipples.

Bhagvata Purana

The fever-goddess enters houses where the divine protector of children—known as Sasthi in Bengal and Satavai in Maharashtra—is not worshipped on the sixth day after the birth of a child:

Priyavarta, son of the patriarch Manu, did not want to marry, but he was compelled by his father to do so. His wife, Malini, did not conceive for many years. After many rituals propitiating the mother-goddess, she became pregnant. But for twelve years she could not deliver the child. After many prayers to the mother-goddess, the child finally emerged but was stillborn. Priyavarta invoked the mother-goddess once again. She appeared in the form of Sasthi. She restored the child to life but refused to give it to Priyavarta until he promised to institute her worship on the sixth day of a child's life.

Folklore from the
state of Bengal

On the sixth day Sasthi enters the house and writes the fate of the child on its forehead with invisible ink. Just as a female cat grabs helpless kittens by the scruff of the neck and keeps them safe from predators, Sasthi fiercely protects infants from fevers when her powers are invoked. Sasthi is therefore closely associated with female cats:

A merchant's wife prepared numerous delicacies for the goddess Sasthi in the hope that her daughter-in-law would bear many healthy children. Leaving her daughter-in-law to guard the food, she went to the river to bathe before making the offering. While she was away, the daughter-in-law could not resist eating the delicacies. When the merchant's wife returned, she discovered that all the plates were empty. "Where did the food go?" "They were eaten by a cat," said the daughter-in-law. This false accusation

made Sasthi very angry, as she loved cats. She decided to teach the liar a lesson. Every time the daughter-in-law delivered a child, Sasthi sent her cat to eat the newborn. When seven babies had been thus killed, the merchant's wife suspected that someone had displeased Sasthi. So she fasted and invoked the goddess, who revealed all. Apologizing for her daughter-in-law, the merchant's wife promised to feed and look after all the cats in her village. This made Sasthi happy, and she brought the seven dead children to life.

Folklore from the
state of West Bengal

The divine child killer is considered the outraged and primal manifestation of the divine child savior:

King Brihadratha of Magadha, who had two queens but no son, chanced upon a magic mango that could make a woman pregnant. Not wanting to play favorites, the king cut the fruit in two and gave one half to each queen. As expected, they became pregnant, but nine months later delivered two lumps of flesh—each, one half of a full child. The lumps of flesh were thrown outside the palace gates, where they were discovered by a flesh-eating ogress called Jara. When she put the two halves together, the child miraculously came to life and began to cry. The boy, thus born, was named Jarasandha after the ogress. The king Brihadratha declared that Jara would no longer be feared in his kingdom as the killer of babies but would be revered in his land as the savior of children. Those who did not revere her would have to face her wrath.

Mahabharata, folklore
from the state of Maharashtra

Though transformed into a child protector, Jara can always revert to her killer form if she is not adored. Her arrival as Jari-Mari is never met with hostility. That can make the situation worse. Instead, she is welcomed and her forgiveness sought. Neem leaves are hung on the doorstep to inform neighbors that the goddess has entered the house. Neem is a medicinal tree with antiseptic and antiviral qualities and is rubbed on the body to reduce itching and secondary infections. When the leaves are put up, women in the neighborhood rush to the temple of Jari-Mari with gifts lest the fiery goddess enter their homes and harm their little ones.

In many parts of India Jari-Mari has no permanent shrine. She roams the countryside with a bag of pox on a donkey accompanied by Jvara, the six-eyed, six-armed, three-headed, three-legged goblin of fever. A small portable shrine to Mari is sometimes carried from village to village by a woman whose husband whips himself while she beats a drum. Mothers whose children are ill reward the man that he may punish himself for their lapses and thus please the angry goddess. If the child survives, it is considered blessed by the goddess; in memory of the goddess who was gracious enough to forgive, the child thus wears a talisman.

A composite shrine to Jari-Mari-Shitala-Sasthi is usually just a rock smeared with red and yellow powder located under a banyan or neem tree outside the village boundaries. The shrine is not maintained by any priest and is often neglected until calamity strikes.

Mothers Who Cause Miscarriage

The shrine of the Matrika mothers is also located in the wilderness, usually on a riverbank or next to a lake, and it is comprised of six to seven vermilion-smeared stones. The Matrikas represent the dark side of water-nymphs. While apsaras seduce sages and give birth to children, the Matrika mothers kill fetuses and newborns unless placated with gifts of bridal finery.

Behind these child-afflicting goddesses is the belief that women who are denied conjugal and maternal bliss vent their frustration by harming children and causing pain to mothers:

Shiva's seed was so powerful that a child born of it could kill the asura Taraka on the seventh day of its life. The devas begged Shiva to give them his seed, but such was its radiance that even the fire-god Agni could not hold it for long. So he cast it into the icy waters of the River Ganga. It so happened that the seven wives of the seven cosmic seers were bathing in these waters. The river water, potent with Shiva's seed, made six of them pregnant. Arundhati, the seventh sage's wife, was so devoted to her husband, Vasistha, that the power of her chastity protected her from succumbing to the water's potency. On learning of the pregnancies, the seven cosmic seers accused the six women of adultery and drove them out. In despair, the women cast out the unwanted embryos from their wombs. The six embryos fell into a marsh and set the reeds ablaze. In the heat of the fire the six embryos fused together and transformed into a radiant child with six heads and twelve arms. When the women heard the child cry, they decided to kill him. However, when they saw the child, milk oozed out of their breasts and they were overwhelmed with maternal affection. They nursed the child. With each of his six heads,

Matrikas, the wild mothers who harm children unless appeased. Relief on wall of Chalukya sanctuary; Aihole, Karnataka. Sixth century.

the child suckled the breasts of his six moth-ers. Because the women were known as Kritikas, the child came to be known as Kartikeya. Kartikeya went on to kill Taraka. When the Kritikas lamented the loss of their marital status and expressed their desire to disrupt pregnancies and kill children—be-cause their fertility was the cause of their misfortune—Kartikeya said, "You are my beloved mothers, the Matrikas. Feel free to harm children of those women who do not revere you as suhagans."

Mahabharata, Skanda Purana

A suhagan is the embodiment of womanly virtue in Hinduism. She represents Nature at her domesticated best. As the chaste, fertile, and loving matriarch whose husband is alive, whose children are healthy, and whose house-hold is prosperous, she is considered auspi-cious, worthy of adoration and reverence. Arundhati, the only wife who did not become pregnant in the above story, is the celestial suhagan.

Once Arundhati along with the Kritikas sat in the celestial sphere alongside their hus-bands, the seven cosmic seers, who form the Great Bear constellation. After their rejection, the Kritikas moved away to form the Pleiades constellation. The chaste Arundhati was al-lowed to remain near the Great Bear as the star Alkor.

To the Hindus, the Arundhati star repre-sents the ideal wife. Its rather faint light is lik-ened to the unawakened desire of the bride. On wedding nights, to help develop intimacy between newlyweds, the groom is advised to play the game "Let's Spot the Arundhati Star" with his wife. "Look at that star," he says, pointing to a bright star not far from Arundhati. As the wife turns to look at it, he caresses her arms, shoulders, and neck, but

then says, "No, that is not Arundhati." He then points to another star and then another and then another, each time going nearer to Arundhati, interspersing each stage with ca-resses on the breasts, waist, navel, each time going nearer and nearer to her pubic area. This progression toward the star is repeated and when the destination is reached, the groom introduces the bride to the mysteries of marriage.

The Kritikas or Matrikas resent Arund-hati's exalted status. Though they are moth-ers, they are not wives, and hence lack social status. Spurned by their husbands on the grounds of infidelity, they have no place in samaja or the civilized world. This makes them eternally jealous of wives and mothers. They transform into wild and ferocious beings wait-ing for an opportunity to overwhelm the do-mesticated realm.

Texts describe the Matrikas as malevolent spirits with long nails, large teeth, shriveled breasts, and protruding lips who lurk outside human settlements, near crossroads, in caves, on hills, in burning grounds, beside riverbanks, near springs, and in forests. Deadly fevers are a manifestation of their rage and resentment. Their frustration abates only when they are offered bridal finery and treated as suhagans.

The Unfulfilled Bride

The idea that to be a suhagan is the ultimate aim of a woman and its denial transforms one into an angry goddess reverberates in folk sto-ries of *devis, matas, ammans,* and other divine females who populate the Indian countryside.

In southern India one comes across temples of Pattini, the chaste wife who became a widow before she could become a mother.

Those responsible for her fate had to pay a terrible price:

Kannagi suffered silently while her husband, Kovalan, spent all his time with a courtesan. When all his money was gone, the courtesan threw Kovalan out of her house. Penniless, Kovalan turned to family and friends for help. They all rejected the philanderer. Only Kannagi stood by him. Together they set out to the city of Madurai to start life afresh. To help Kovalan raise capital for his business, Kannagi gave him one of her gold anklets. When Kovalan offered this anklet for sale in the market, the goldsmiths accused him of stealing the queen's jewelry. They took him to the king, who ordered his immediate execution. When Kannagi learned how her husband had been put to death, she strode into the royal palace, presented her other anklet, proved her husband's innocence, and demanded justice. "Give me back my husband," she cried. When there was no response, she plucked off one of her breasts and hurled it into the city square. Instantly the whole city of Madurai was engulfed in flames. All its residents—who had stood silently by while Kannagi's innocent husband was being put to death—were burnt alive. Tales of how Kannagi destroyed the city of Madurai spread across the countryside. Residents of neighboring villages enshrined her images in temples and began worshipping her as a goddess.

Shilappadikaram

Kannagi's power to destroy an entire city comes from her bottled-up creative energy. With her husband, she would have used this energy to produce babies and make a home. Without him, her festering creative energy transforms into destructive energy. The mother thus becomes a killer.

Another woman transformed into a killer-goddess after her husband rejected her:

The sage Jaratkaru married Manasi, the sister of Vasuki, king of serpents. She served him dutifully. One day he took a siesta, placing his head on her lap. Hours passed. Jaratkaru showed no signs of waking up, and Manasi remained rooted to the spot, not wanting to move or wake him up. As the sun was about to set, Manasi realized it was time for her husband to perform the evening rituals. If he did not do it on time, he could risk the wrath of nocturnal spirits. So with great hesitation, she roused her husband from his peaceful slumber. Jaratkaru was furious. "How dare you wake me up? I would have woken up on my own to perform the ritual on time." Because Manasi had broken the vow of total obedience, Jaratkaru abandoned her.

Mahabharata

Divorced women, though unwidowed, are not quite suhagans. Though she bears a child, Manasi's rejection by her husband prevents her from attaining the exalted status of a matriarch. In her quest for dignity, Manasi demands worship by sending serpents that kill those who disregard her existence. The tale of the goddess of snakebites, also known as Manasa, is popular in the eastern state of Bengal:

The goddess Manasa appeared before a merchant and demanded that he worship her. The merchant worshipped only Shiva and ignored Manasa's demand. Furious, the goddess de-

stroyed his ships and reduced him to abject poverty. Then, appearing as a damsel, she won his heart. But she refused to make love to him until he began worshipping Manasa. The merchant preferred breaking up with her to worshipping the goddess of snakes. Finally, Manasa sent her serpents to bite and kill the merchant's only son on his wedding night. She promised to revive him only if the merchant offered flowers at her temple. The merchant gave in. The goddess was pleased and the merchant's son came back to life.

Folklore from the
state of Bengal

One little-known folk goddess brings joy only when she is given gifts of bridal finery because she lost the opportunity to be a bride:

A king once saw a beautiful girl in the fields. Overwhelmed by desire, he ordered her to come to the royal garden at night bedecked as a bride. To save her honor, her twin brother went in her place dressed as a woman. The sister saw the king make love to her brother. The deed hardly seemed dishonorable. She saw the passion in the king's face and joy in her brother's eyes. Feeling deprived and rejected, she transformed into a fiery goddess, raised her sword, killed the king and her brother, and took refuge in the forest.

Folklore from the
state of Tamil Nadu

Wives of Homosexual Men

To the east of India, in the state of Gujarat, is

the temple of Bahuchera, who is the patron goddess of eunuchs, transvestites, and cross-dressing homosexuals. She is described as riding a brightly colored Indian rooster. There are many legends associated with her. In each she is deprived of the pleasures of being a wife:

Bahuchera was on her way to a fair when she was attacked by a thief called Bapiya. To save herself from abduction and rape, she cut her breasts. As she bled to death, she cursed her attacker: "May you become impotent." When Bapiya begged for mercy, she said, "You will attain salvation only if you build a temple in my honor and live in it dressed as a woman." Since that day, impotent men, hermaphrodites, transsexuals, and transvestites have worshipped the goddess Bahuchera, believing that their sexuality that prevents them from marrying women and having a family is the result of offending women in the past life.

Folklore from the
state of Gujarat

In another story the goddess laments her fate when she discovers that her husband is incapable of having sex with her:

Once a prince did not want to get married. But his parents forced him to tie the knot with a beautiful princess. Every night the princess waited for her groom, but he would not come to her bed. Instead, he would ride into the forest on his horse. The princess decided to investigate and followed the prince. Because she had no horse, she rode a rooster and came upon a clearing in the forest, where she found her

husband having sex with other men. *"Why then did you marry me and ruin my life if you do not desire women?"* she asked angrily. She then cut off his genitals. Her fury and unfulfilled desire transformed her into the goddess Bahuchera. The prince wore women's clothes and worshipped her, praying for his salvation.

Folklore from the
state of Gujarat

The goddess fumes with sexual frustration. She often appears in the dreams of men, usually homosexuals, and demands that they castrate themselves, dress up as women, and serve her in her temple. Thus the goddess protects women from being tricked into sterile unions.

Homosexuality represents another manifestation of Nature's unfathomable secrets that confounds samaja. It appears with unfailing regularity within the square of civilization. The female homosexual does not disrupt the social edifice, as female arousal is not necessary for conception and the lesbian's desire can be hidden or brutally suppressed in the patriarch's harem. But the male homosexual poses a problem. Though part of the wheel of existence, his biological urges do not help rotate the cycle of life. He is capable of performing his social duties but incapable of fulfilling his biological obligations. A nymph can at least seduce the heterosexual ascetic. She fails before the homosexual householder. In ancient India such a man had two options. He could live within society, marry, and—for children—practice *levirate*, inviting a brother or priest to impregnate his wife. Or he could leave home, castrate himself, don female apparel, suffer the burden of his karma, and worship goddesses in the hope of being born a heterosexual in his next life.

There is no such word as *homosexual* in the Indian vocabulary. Words such as *kliba* or *napunsaka*—which, roughly translated, mean "not quite a man"—are used in a derogatory manner for men incapable of fulfilling their biological obligation because of a physical defect or mental quirk. The social engineers who wrote the Dharmashastras, unable to find a place for male homosexuals within the heterosexual scheme of things, treated them with derision. They were not allowed to participate in religious ceremonies or inherit property.

All across India there are isolated communities of feminine men known as *hijras*. These are a mixture of hermaphrodites, transsexuals, eunuchs, and cross-dressing homosexuals. They are treated with a mixture of fear, disgust, and sympathy. Samaja tolerates their existence on the fringes of civilization, where Nature and society intermingle. Some serve in brothels and in women's apartments as cooks, cleaners, and catamites. Others live celibate lives in temples. They become priestesses of the goddess, sharing her frustration at being unable to share the joys of the household. They are invited to drive away malevolent spirits with their song and dance. They are invited to wedding ceremonies and to houses of barren women to sing, dance, invoke the goddess, and usher in fertility. They visit houses soon after a child is born to check its genitals. If all is normal, they congratulate the patriarch's fortune and demand gifts that become their means of livelihood. If the genitals are misshapen, they take the child away and raise it as a hijra. The child is thus saved from social ignominy and certain death.

Though tales with homosexual themes are extremely rare in sacred Hindu lore, cross-dressing is commonly resorted to by heroes to beguile their enemies:

Draupadi, wife of the five Pandava brothers,

who had been publicly humiliated by Duryodhana, the Kaurava, vowed not to braid her hair until she could use Duryodhana's thighbone as her comb. She was told that the defeat of Duryodhana would be possible only if her husbands obtained a sacred whip, sword, drum, casket, and lamp belonging to a warlord called Gurulingam. To get these sacred artifacts, Arjuna, Draupadi's favorite husband, approached Gurulingam's son Pormannan disguised as a beautiful girl called Vijayampal and enticed him with her charms. Pormannan agreed to kill his own father, Gurulingam, and give Vijayampal the sacred objects of worship if she became his wife. But when the deed was done and the gifts given, Poramannan was shocked to find that his beloved Vijayampal was a man! Undaunted, he demanded the Pandavas give him a wife, as Arjuna had aroused his hunger but left him unsatiated. They gave him their younger sister, Cankuvati. Poramannan became the guardian of his sister-in-law Draupadi and helped her forces defeat Duryodhana.

Folklore from the
state of Tamil Nadu

Tales of men dressing as women are far more common than tales of women dressing as men.

Metal head of the goddess Renuka-Yellamma, placed on rims of earthenware pots and wicker baskets to create an effigy of the mother-goddess. Twentieth century.

Auspicious Harlots

Society tries its best to bridle the sexual urge and restrain it to the childbearing process. Yet occasionally, the full force of sexual desire makes itself felt. Adulterous desires cause a suhagan to risk all that society holds dear. The rejected adulteress transforms into the divine patron of harlots, who absorb the unbridled lust of men that could otherwise disrupt social order:

Ordered by his father, Parashurama beheaded his mother, Renuka, who had experienced adulterous thoughts after looking upon a gandharva. Pleased with this display of unquestioning obedience, the sage Jamadagni

offered Parashurama a boon. He demanded his mother be restored to life. "Bring me her head and I will rejoin it to her body," said Jamadagni. However, Parashurama could not find the head. "In that case, find me the head of another woman who parts with it willingly," said Jamadagni. Parashurama roamed the world and found Yellamma, a low-caste woman, who agreed to be beheaded so that Renuka may live. Pleased with Yellamma's sacrifice, Parashurama, who was Vishnu incarnate, declared that she would be worshipped as a goddess.

Folklore from the states of
Andhra Pradesh, Karnataka,
and Maharashtra

In another version of the story, there is a misplacement of heads:

When Parashurama raised his ax to behead Renuka, she ran and took refuge in the house of a low-caste woman called Yellamma. Yellamma tried to stop Parashurama from killing Renuka by coming between mother and son. Parashurama swung his ax anyway and beheaded both women. Later the sage Jamadagni gave Parashurama a pot of magic water to revive both women. In his hurry to restore his mother to life, he exchanged the heads of the two women. Thus he put Renuka's head on Yellamma's body and Yellamma's head on Renuka's body. When this was realized, Jamadagni accepted the woman with the chaste head and high-caste body as his wife. The woman with the unchaste head and a low-caste body became a goddess.

Folklore from the states of
Andhra Pradesh, Karnataka,
and Maharashtra

Renuka means "soil maiden." *Yellamma* means "everybody's mother." She is the benevolent earth mother, free from the fence of matrimony, who accepts all seeds without discrimination. Women known as *devadasis*, "servants of god," carry a metal effigy of her head attached to the rim of a basket or pot. As diminutive doubles of the goddess, these women have no husbands; they make themselves available to whoever desires them sexually. This, society hopes, satisfies the potential rapist and protects the edifice of family life based on female chastity.

The devadasis live on alms. Their children have no father and no lineage. Girls, like their mothers, are dedicated to the goddess. Boys are also turned into devadasis, made to wear female apparel and serve as catamites. The boys are known as *jogatis*. Like the goddess, who was rejected by her husband, they are social outcasts. Right from birth they are made to believe that marriage and family life is not for them, and that their role as prostitutes is vital in the scheme of civilization. The exploitation of devadasis, who mostly belong to the lower socioeconomic strata of society, is a major sociopolitical issue today.

Courtesans have always been part of Hindu civilization. Hundreds of women once served as sacred prostitutes in the great temple complexes of southern India. They were given in marriage to the presiding deity, and they entertained the idol with performances in the great dance hall located right in front of the sanctum sanctorum. Because they never became widows, they were adored as sada suhagans, eternal brides.

The public wives or courtesans of ancient Hindu society were also highly cultured and educated women. Trained in sixty-four ways to arouse the mind and the senses, these women were considered earthly manifestations of celestial damsels. Rich and powerful men sought them as mistresses. They gradually became symbols of power and fortune. Because beauty, wealth, and luxury always surrounded them, they were considered especially blessed by Laxmi, goddess of fortune. Mud from brothels was used while laying down the foundations of a new house to usher in prosperity. This mud was also used to make idols of the mother-goddess. These women were considered auspicious because they never became widows and were hence eternally lucky *akhanda sowbhagyavatis*. Merchants preferred to look upon their faces before setting out with their caravans. They were invited to wedding ceremonies to tie the marriage thread known as *mangalasutra* around the wife's neck, to wish her happiness, and to bless her that she may never know the fate of a widow.

Liberating the Hair

Widowhood in India is considered a terrible fate. When the husband dies, a woman becomes an inauspicious widow. The red dot on her forehead is wiped off. Her bangles are broken. Her bright clothes are removed. Shorn of flowers and jewelry, she is draped in white robes and made to live in isolation, unseen by male eyes. Traditionally, even her head was shaved.

Many believe that a widow is made unattractive for her own good to protect her from rapists. With her husband gone, there is no one to protect her honor. But husbands are not always capable of protecting their wives:

❀

Yudhishtira, the eldest of the five Pandava brothers, gambled away his kingdom, his brothers, himself, and finally their common wife, Draupadi, to their archenemies, the Kauravas. The Kauravas dragged Draupadi by the hair into the gambling hall and decided to humiliate the proud Pandava queen by disrobing her in public. This happened during Draupadi's menstrual period. Bound by the rules of the game and the laws of civilization, none of the kings, warriors, and noblemen assembled in the Kaurava court came to Draupadi's rescue. She stood there bleeding, naked, with hair unbound, seething with fury. Through tearful bloodshot eyes, she looked at her five husbands, who hung their heads in shame. The laws of dharma had failed in their promise to protect her. Man had abused her and would pay a terrible price. In her fury, Draupadi took an oath that she would not tie her hair until she had washed it with the blood of Kauravas.

Mahabharata

In the traditional retelling of the Mahabharata Draupadi is not disrobed. As the Kaurava Dushasana tugs on Draupadi's sari, he pulls out several hundred yards of cloth, and the sari is never undone. The miracle is attributed to Krishna, who is guardian of dharma and Vishnu incarnate. When Duryodhana orders Draupadi to sit on his left thigh—a place reserved for wives and concubines—the Pandava Bhima loses his temper and swears to break Duryodhana's thigh. All this does not stop Draupadi from taking her vow to wash her hair in blood. In one Tamil folk version of the Mahabharata, Draupadi's vow is more fierce, more dark. "I will wash my hair in Dushasana's blood. I will comb it with Duryodhana's hair. With Kaurava entrails will I tie it up, and with their hearts I will decorate it." As this vow is

Draupadi being disrobed in public by the Kauravas, while her husbands, the Pandavas, watch helplessly. Twentieth century calendar art.

had gone for her bath and was not ready to receive it. The impatient Upayaja poured the water into the fire altar. Out came a beautiful woman called Draupadi.

Mahabharata

In the epic Krishna strikes a deal, and the Kauravas promise to return the Pandava kingdom after they spend thirteen years in the forest. At the end of the period of exile, the Kauravas go back on their words. This leads to a terrible war on the fields of Kurukshetra with echoes of the celestial battles between the devas and the asuras. Bhima kills each and every Kaurava and helps Draupadi wash her hair in blood. He even drinks blood, thus taking the role of Bhairava, the minion of the primal goddess.

In classical versions, during the thirteen-year exile, Draupadi's unbound hair constantly reminds her husbands of how they failed her as husbands. It indicates to the Pandavas that they have lost their marital rights over their common wife.

Hair has traditionally been used as the symbol of femininity in general and fertility in particular. Plaited hair, without flowers, represents the dormant fertility of a prepubescent virgin. Plaited hair with flowers represents the roused fertility of an unmarried girl. Parted hair with the parting smeared with red powder known as *kumkum* acknowledges a woman's realized fertility and her domestication by marriage. The shaved heads of widows and of nuns represent fertility that is crushed. Unbound hair represents free and wild fertility, unrestrained by any man. It is the hair of *kumari*, the divine warrior maiden.

voiced, Draupadi with unbound hair appears less like the royal matriarch, queen of Indraprastha, wife of the five Pandavas, and mother of their five sons. She seems more a killer-goddess. The Kauravas transform into demons, the Pandavas into gods, with Krishna doing for them what Vishnu does for devas.

Draupadi is no ordinary woman in the epic. She was not conceived as mortals are:

King Drupada invited the sage Upayaja to perform a yagna and produce water potent enough to conceive a powerful child. When the water was prepared, Drupada's queen

Widow by Choice

Despite the low status of widows in Hindu society, one woman killed her own husband and transformed into a goddess:

A sweeper fell in love with Dayamava, the daughter of a priest. Posing as a priest, he married her and brought her to his mother's house. Unaware that her husband was a low-caste sweeper, the high-caste Dayamava served him with devotion and bore him many children. One day, during dinner, her mother-in-law remarked that the food tasted like cow's tongue. Dayamava recoiled in horror, because only sweepers eat the carcasses of cows. Priests are supposed to be vegetarians. Realizing she had been duped by her husband, Dayamava raised a sickle, killed her mother-in-law and her children, and burnt the house. In fear, her husband ran out in the form of a male buffalo. Dayamava chased him, caught him by the horns, pinned him down with her foot, and beheaded him.

Folklore from the
state of Karnataka

Dayamava is a village goddess known by many names in southern India. In annual festivals her buffalo husband—decorated with neem leaves, turmeric, and vermilion powder—is sacrificed before her shrine and her widowhood reenacted. The red dot on her forehead is wiped off, her bangles are broken, and her *magalasutra*, the auspicious necklace of a bride, is pulled away. However, her hair is not shaved off. It is simply left unbound as she transforms into an autonomous warrior-goddess.

The most popular warrior-goddess of sacred Hindu lore is Durga:

The buffalo-demon Mahisha could be killed only by a woman. Unable to defeat him in battle, Indra and the devas led by Vishnu went to Brahma, the creator, and requested him to create a woman who would kill Mahisha. Brahma led all the gods to Shiva on Mount Kailas. Shiva, roused out of his meditation by the pandemonium caused by Mahisha, swelled with wrath. His rage poured forth as fire from his mouth. The other gods, who stood around him, also opened their mouths and let loose their unrestrained powers as sheets and streams of flame. The fires rushed together, combining in a flaming cloud that grew and grew and ultimately condensed into a ball of blinding light, out of which emerged a magnificent goddess with many arms called Durga. Armed with weapons given to her by the devas, the goddess rode into battle on a lion and challenged Mahisha to a combat. The asura came onto the battlefield and, roused by her beauty, proposed marriage. The goddess laughed and promised to marry him if he could defeat her in duel. In the fight that followed Mahisha attacked Durga in the form of an elephant, a lion, and finally a buffalo. She defeated him each time. Finally she caught hold of the buffalo-demon's horns, smote him with her tender feet, pinned him to the ground with her trident, and beheaded him with her scimitar.

Devi Bhagvatam

The stories of Dayamava and Durga are remarkably similar. In both a woman kills a buffalo. While in the Dayamava story the pro-

Durga, the virgin warrior-goddess, battling the buffalo-demon.
Stone carving; Mamallapuram, Tamil Nadu. Seventh century.

tagonist is a mortal woman and the buffalo is her husband, in the Durga story the protagonist is a goddess and the buffalo, a demon who harasses the gods. In both stories the female character turns wild and dangerous after being liberated from male control. Dayamava shrugs off her husband's marital right obtained through trickery. Durga comes into being when the gods let loose their wild energies, their shaktis, confined and restrained within their physical frame. Dayamava decides of her own free will that her husband must die. Durga, on the other hand, is created by the gods and instructed to kill the buffalo-demon who troubles them. In both stories romance is shredded violently. Dayamava kills her hus-

band on discovering that he had seduced her with a lie. Durga kills Mahisha incensed by his proposal of marriage.

Many scholars believe that Durga is the polished and patriarchal version of a primal matriarchal goddess. In Himachal Pradesh, a state in northern India, a buffalo-god known as Mahasu is worshipped by villagers as a manifestation of Shiva. In the western state of Maharashtra, too, Mhasoba, the buffalo father, is a folk god identified with Shiva.

Some classical Hindu scriptures do suggest that the buffalo-demon could be in some way related to Shiva:

When Durga severed Mahisha's neck, she found a linga within. In his past life Mahisha was a devotee of Shiva, but a curse turned him into a buffalo. While grazing, he accidentally swallowed a linga that stuck in his throat.

Skanda Purana

In other classical Hindu texts Mahisha's ungodly origins are stressed:

The asura Rambha made love to a female buffalo named Mahishi and brought her to the nether regions as his wife. The asuras, disgusted by the union of demon and beast, drove them out. Eventually Mahishi gave birth to the buffalo-demon Mahisha. Soon after, Mahishi caught the eye of a wild male buffalo who gored his rival Rambha to death. In despair, Mahishi killed herself on her husband's funeral pyre. The lovesick male buffalo drowned himself. The orphaned Mahisha performed austerities and invoked Brahma, who bestowed upon him the boon of dying only at the hands of a woman. Believing women to be too weak to fight, Mahisha assumed his invincibility. He raised an army of asuras and drove the devas out of Amravati.

Vamana Purana

Prepubescent Divinity

Shiva is popularly believed to be Durga's consort. But the goddess is never depicted sitting beside him as a demure wife. Her name,

Durga—meaning "inaccessible, unconquerable one"—acknowledges her autonomy. She is often called kumari, which is generally translated to mean "virgin." But as the manifestation of Parvati, whose lovemaking with Shiva sustains the universe, Durga can hardly be considered a virgin. Perhaps *kumari* simply means "unattached to a man." As a consort, a goddess is largely a mother. In autonomy, she turns into a killer.

Often a warrior-goddess is not just kumari. She is also *kanya*, a prepubescent girl. The patron goddess of the kingdom of Nepal known as Taleju is a kumari and a kanya:

The king of Nepal invited the goddess Taleju, guardian of his kingdom, to a game of dice. As they played, the king looked upon her with eyes of desire. Enraged, the goddess disappeared, leaving the borders of Nepal open to all intruders. The king begged for mercy. Finally, the goddess promised to protect Nepal so long as the king worshipped her in the form of a prepubescent girl who does not arouse sexual desires.

Folklore from
the kingdom of Nepal

Every few years, under orders of the Hindu monarch of Nepal, premenstrual girls from the family of goldsmiths are made to witness the slaughtering of male buffaloes. Girls who witness it without showing any sign of fear are considered manifestations of the goddess. One of them is enshrined in the temple and worshipped by the king himself. The child-goddess loses her divinity as soon as she menstruates.

Goddesses never menstruate. Menstrual blood contains their power. When they sit beside a male god, this power is domesticated.

Beside Shiva, Parvati is demure and maternal. Without the male god, however, the power becomes destructive energy that the gods direct toward their enemies:

From the bodies of the gods emerged their shaktis in female form. Vaishnavi emerged from Vishnu, holding a discus, riding an eagle. Shivani emerged from Shiva, bearing a trident, riding a bull. Brahmani emerged from Brahma, holding a rosary, riding a swan. Kaumari emerged from Kumara, holding a lance, riding a peacock. Indrani emerged from Indra, holding a bow, riding an elephant. The lion woman Narasimhi emerged out of the lion man Narasimha. The wild sow Varahi emerged from the wild boar Varaha. Together these seven warrior women tore down the demon army, killed all the asuras, and drank their blood.

Vamana Purana, Devi Bhagvatam

The power of the gods is domesticated within their male forms. When released, they transform into a terrifying horde of wild goddesses. These warrior-goddesses are always shown as autonomous beings who surround and serve the great goddess.

When the gods need the help of a woman in their battles against the demons, they prevent her from getting married, fearing that matrimony and maternity will tame her power and render her useless as a warrior:

Punyakshi wanted to marry Shiva, but the gods would not permit it because only as a virgin did Punyakshi have the power to kill demons. To thwart her marriage plans, they declared that only a man who could give Punyakshi's father a betel leaf without veins, a sugarcane without rings, and a coconut without eyes could claim her as his wife. In answer to Punyakshi's prayer, Shiva conjured these gifts and became the chosen groom. Punyakshi's father began wedding preparations and sent for the astrologer to determine an auspicious hour for the marriage ceremony. "She can marry this very night or at the end of time," said the astrologer, who was in fact Indra in disguise. Shiva immediately set out from his mountainous abode in the north of India. Punyakshi's village stood on the southern tip of the continent. The journey was a long one, and the gods were confident Shiva would not make it. But Shiva used his powers and covered the distance rapidly. Fearing he would make it to the wedding, Indra took the form of a rooster and began to crow in the middle of the night. Tricked into thinking that it was daybreak and the auspicious hour of marriage had passed, Shiva turned around. When dawn came and there was no sign of the groom, the wedding guests departed. Frustrated, Punyakshi kicked the pots of food prepared for the wedding banquet. These turned into grains of sand. She washed her face in the sea and the cosmetics colored the sea. Demons mocked her fate and proposed marriage. In her rage, Punyakshi picked up her sickle and killed them all. Punyakshi then stood on the southern tip of India and decided to wait for Shiva until the end of time. She became renowned as the goddess Kanyakumari, the virgin goddess.

Kanyakumari Sthala Purana

Another goddess used her virginal powers to kill the man who tried to rape her:

Trikuta wanted to marry Rama, prince of Ayodhya. But Rama was married to Sita and he refused to take a second wife. So Trikuta became a nun and lived an ascetic life. One day a Tantrik, Bhairo, visited her house and asked for food. In keeping with the laws of hospitality, she served him a meal. Bhairo objected to the vegetarian food placed before him. He also demanded sex and wine. When Trikuta refused, Bhairo tried to molest her. Trikuta ran out of the hermitage. Bhairo pursued her. Trikuta's companion, a monkey, tried to stop him but failed. Finally tired of running, Trikuta turned on her pursuer. She raised her sword and beheaded him. As his head was severed, Bhairo pleaded for mercy and acknowledged her as the primal mother. Trikuta accepted him as her child.

Folklore from the
state of Jammu

Trikuta is worshipped as Vaishnavi in the Jammu valley to the north of India. Unlike most warrior-goddesses, who are considered manifestations of Shiva's consort, Vaishnavi is linked to Vishnu, hence vegetarian. This makes her unique, because most warrior-goddesses receive blood sacrifice of male animals.

Virgin Mother

Taleju, Punyakshi, Durga, and Dayamava are all considered manifestations of Parvati and are referred to as *kumari-matas*, virgin mothers. But the goddess Parvati is neither a virgin nor a mother, at least not in the conventional sense of the term. Her womb never bears fruit.

Her lovemaking with Shiva sustains the universe. The gods wanted her to get married so that Shiva would father a child. Interestingly, they prevent Parvati from accepting that seed in her womb:

The gods wanted Shiva to father a child who would help them defeat demons. The goddess Parvati succeeded in winning Shiva as a husband. As they made love, the gods knew that Parvati would milk out Shiva's semen, but they did not want her to get pregnant. "Born of Shiva's seed and nurtured in Parvati's womb, the child will be more powerful than Indra," said the devas. So they sent the fire-god Agni to disturb the love play of the divine couple. Agni took the form of a bird and entered their cave. Embarrassed by the intrusion, the goddess turned away from Shiva, and Shiva spurted his seed into the fire-god's mouth. Out of this seed was born Kartikeya, commander of the celestial armies.

Kalika Purana, Brahmanda Purana,
Vamana Purana

The gods fear that Shiva's child by Parvati will be more powerful than them. So they transfer Shiva's seed into another womb, but its radiance is too strong for anyone to bear. Neither the fire-god Agni nor the river-goddess Ganga can hold it for long. So it is split into six parts, nurtured in the wombs of the six Kritika maidens, and ultimately transformed into a six-headed divine warlord named Kartikeya after the Kritikas. Another reason that the gods do not want Parvati to bear a child, perhaps, is that maternity will drain her power and prevent her from transforming into a killer-goddess.

Parvati is so furious at being unable to realize her maternal potential that she curses the gods:

The goddess made love to Shiva in the hope of bearing his child. But her love play was disturbed and the gods took away Shiva's seed. In her rage, Parvati cursed the gods that they would never have children.

Brahmavaivarta Purana

Parvati wants to be a mother but Shiva tells her, "I am an ascetic and do not wish to be burdened with children or family. I am immortal, have no ancestors, and need no sons to offer oblations to dead forefathers or to continue my lineage." Still, the goddess wants a child, so she bears one without a husband. The child thus born is called Vinayaka, "he who was conceived without a man":

Shiva refused to give Parvati a child, so she created one on her own. She anointed her skin with oil and turmeric, scraped it off, and molded Vinayaka out of it. She ordered him to guard her cave and prevent all from entering it. Vinayaka—who had never before seen his mother's consort—stopped Shiva from entering Parvati's abode. Enraged, Shiva raised his trident and beheaded his son. When Parvati saw her son's headless body, she was so angry that her anger turned into ferocious yoginis who threatened to destroy the entire cosmos. To appease his consort, Shiva revived Vinayaka by replacing his severed head with that of an elephant. He acknowledged the resurrected child as the first of his followers, Ganapati.

Shiva Purana, Vamana Purana

Tales of autonomous women who bear children without male help is also found in tribal lore:

A man had five daughters. While four of them wanted husbands and children, the youngest wanted only children, no husband. The four elder girls turned into the mango, tamarind, fig, and berry trees; the youngest girl, Kadali, turned into a plantain—a plant that many believe produces fruits parthogenically without any cross-pollination or involvement of birds and bees.

Tribal lore from central India

The plantain is a sacred plant used to mark the corners of any sacred altar. It is seen as the symbol of the autonomous creative energy of the goddess.

Chaste Guardians

The idea that the son loves and protects the mother more than her husband does is very strong in India:

Vinata, mother of birds, and Kadru, mother of serpents, were two wives of the sage Kashyapa. Vinata believed that the divine horse Ucchaishrava was spotlessly white. Kadru believed it had a black tail. Vinata was so confident that she was right that she told Kadru, "If you can prove that Ucchaishrava's tail is black, not white, then I will be your slave." Kadru ordered her children, the serpents, to cling to the tail of the divine horse as it rode past the horizon at dawn the next day so that it appeared to have a black tail from afar. By this deceit, Kadru won the wager and made Vinata her slave, demanding divine nectar, as the price of her freedom. Garuda, mightiest of Vinata's sons, fought the gods, stole the pot of nectar, and secured the release of his mother. Before Kadru or any serpent could take a sip of the divine drink, Garuda helped Indra steal the nectar back. Because his mother had been enslaved by the mother of serpents, Garuda became the eternal enemy of serpents and made them his natural food.

Mahabharata

Parvati creates Ganapati not only to satisfy her maternal instincts but also because only a son, she believes, will obey her without question. She orders Ganapati to keep out all those who encroach on her space. Ganapati obeys to the point of preventing even her consort from entering her cave at the risk of certain death. Ganapati is therefore considered the lord of thresholds, to be invoked before the start of any activity or journey. At one time he was feared, because he could put obstacles in the path of those who did not appease him. Nowadays he is adored as a god who helps his devotees attain their goals. Ganapati sits on the threshold of all knowledge and wealth. Whoever seeks to explore the mysteries of his mother needs to seek his permission. In southern India, where Ganapati is considered celibate, it is said that he refused to marry because he found no woman as beautiful as his mother.

Besides her son, the autonomous warrior-goddess has other male doorkeepers who do not look upon her sexually. These include the celibate Hanuman—the monkey-god known in northern India as *langoor-devata*—and the childlike Bhairava. Interestingly, both are considered

manifestations of Shiva and protect the goddess from those who seek to violate her. Hanuman helped release Sita from the clutches of Ravana. Bhairava beheaded Brahma, who had cast his lustful eyes on the goddess:

When Brahma created the primal mother, he pursued her relentlessly to satisfy his lust. Shiva transformed into Bhairava, wrenched off Brahma's fifth head, and stopped the pursuit. But the head seared into Bhairava's flesh and drove him mad. He sought refuge with the goddess, whose maternal grace cured him. He became her eternal protector.

Bhavishya Purana

Bhairava is always portrayed as a child holding a scimitar in one hand and a human head said to be that of Brahma in the other hand. As the wild minion of the goddess, he joins her in battle when she takes the form of Korravai, or he transforms into the goblin of fever Juara when she takes the form of Jari-Mari. He is also seen in the company of Matrika mothers.

Autonomous warrior-goddesses are also attended by groups of women, who, like them, are not associated with men. These women are known as yoginis (who are virginal), *matrikas* (who are maternal), and *dakinis* (who are withered crones). These women are unrestrained, wild, sexual, and violent. They are feared, not adored.

Wild Killer

By preventing Parvati from becoming a mother in the conventional way, the gods ensure that her raw power seethes within her, ready to manifest itself for the benefit of the world:

The gods could not kill Raktabija. Every drop of his blood gave rise to another Raktabija until the entire battlefield would swarm with Raktabija clones. So they invoked Shiva's consort, and she appeared on the battlefield as Kali, the dark one. She rolled out her tongue and covered the battlefield, licking every drop of Raktabija's blood before it touched the ground. Thus no new Raktabija duplicates were created, and the gods were able to kill the dreaded demon.

Devi Bhagvatam,
Vamana Purana

Only the wild goddess can achieve the impossible and defeat apparently invincible demons:

The gods could not defeat the demons, because their guru Shukra kept reviving the fallen warriors with the power of mantra. They sought the help of Shiva, but Shiva refused to kill a man who belonged to the caste of priests. Instead, out of his third eye came a ferocious goddess with flowing hair, a great belly, pendulous breasts, thighs like plantain tree trunks, and a mouth like a great cavern. There were teeth and eyes in her womb. The goddess ran after Shukra, grabbed him, stripped him of his clothes, embraced him, and finally locked him in her womb. With Shukra trapped, the gods were able to kill the demons with ease and win the celestial battle.

Kalika Purana

In her wild, autonomous state, the sexual and violent urges of the goddess are unbridled:

The demon Ruru with this army attacked the gods, who sought refuge with Devi. Devi laughed, and from her mouth emerged an army of goddesses, who wiped out the demon army. After the battle, the goddesses were hungry and demanded food. "Let us eat Shiva, who smells like a goat," said the goddesses. Shiva suggested that they eat all that pregnant women have defiled with their touch, fetuses, newborns, and women who cry all the time. The goddesses refused to eat such food. So Shiva finally offered them his testicles. This satisfied the goddesses, who saluted Shiva.

Padma Purana, Linga Purana,
Matsya Purana

Restraining the Virgin

While the destructive power of Kali is necessary to destroy demons, once the deed is done, her power needs to be restrained and transformed into creative power. Domestication of her divine energies is vital, because they have the capacity to overrun civilization. This is achieved through marriage:

Drunk in blood, Kali loses all good sense, running amok and destroying everything in her path. To stop her, Shiva lay in her path with penis erect. When Kali stepped on Shiva's body, his handsome face aroused desire in her body. She remembered that she

The fierce and untamed Kali stepping on her consort, Shiva, as she sets about destroying the world.
Patta painting, folk style from Orissa. Twentieth century.

was Parvati, and the body she had kicked was that of her husband. Embarrassed, she bit her tongue. She made love to Shiva's corpse and revived her husband. She then sat beside him as a demure consort.

Linga Purana

Maternity also domesticates the goddess:

Shiva took the form of an infant and began to cry. The cry of the baby evoked maternal desires in Kali's heart. She picked up the child and began nursing him. Gradually, her rage dissipated. She regained control of her mind and, in the form of Parvati, rejoined Shiva atop Mount Kailas.

Folklore from the states
of Bengal and Tamil Nandu

The taming power of matrimony is a recurrent theme in sacred Hindu lore:

Meenakshi, princess of Madurai, was born with three breasts and a very masculine temperament. As soon as she ascended the throne after her father's death, she set out with her armies to conquer the world. All the kings who opposed her ambitions were either defeated or killed. Finally, she reached Mount Kailas. The resident ascetic refused to accept her suzerainty. Furious, she challenged him to a duel. But no sooner did she cast her eyes on him than she fell in love. Instantly her extra breast disappeared and she became a demure maiden who accepted the ascetic as her consort. Her brother Vishnu, lord of civilization, gave her away in marriage.

Madurai Sthala Purana

Meenakshi's third breast represents her independent spirit, which goes away when she falls in love. Sometimes the goddess needs to be shamed into submission:

To subjugate Kali, Shiva challenged her to a dance competition. The goddess danced as well as the god, matching him step for step. But then Shiva raised his foot to take the pose known as urdva nataraja. Overwhelmed by modesty, Kali refused to raise her foot and expose her genitals. Thus was her arrogance curbed and her humility aroused. She bent her head and shyly sat on Shiva's left thigh.

Temple legend from
the state of Tamil Nadu

The male head recoils in horror at the stark nakedness of Kali. Offerings of *chunari* and *choli*, "veils" and "blouses," are made to cover the nakedness of the goddess and to domesticate her. The goddess, in turn, demands male heads in sacrifice.

A Bowl Full of Blood

Kali, the wild and fierce goddess of the forest, was once the patron of thieves and marauders, tribes that lived outside the pale of civilization and earned their living by breaking the law and through plunder. They justified their killing as a ritual to satisfy her divine bloodlust:

A caravan traveling through the forest was ambushed by forest tribes. They stole the

Three forms of the mother-goddess, embodying her totality: Kali (left) seated on corpses and feeding on human entrails; Lakshmi (center) holding a lotus as she brings forth the beauty and bounty of Nature; Durga (right) bearing weapons as she protects all life.
Idols from Kailasnatha temple; Ellora, Maharasthra. Seventh century.

goods, raped the women, dragged young men to the altar of the goddess Kali, and beheaded them. When they left, one woman who had hidden herself under an overturned cart discovered the decapitated body of her husband. She lamented her fate. Holding his head in her hands, she sat before the image of the goddess and refused to move or eat until the goddess had restored her husband to life. After seven nights, pleased with the widow's devotion and determination, the goddess appeared. She brought her husband back to life and blessed the couple.

Folklore from the state of Punjab

In Hindu rituals uncooked fruits and nuts are offered to please Shiva. Sweet food cooked in clarified butter is offered to Vishnu. Only the goddess is offered blood sacrifice. The beheading of male animals—buffaloes, goats, and cocks—pleases her. Killing a female animal arouses her wrath. At one time humans were sacrificed, too. Temple lore is full of tales of devotees who beheaded themselves to please the goddess. Nowadays blood sacrifice is frowned upon. Coconuts are broken or lemons and pumpkins cut instead. Some see the cutting of pumpkins and lemons as symbolic of castration. Others see the cracking of the coconut as the destruction of the male ego that is responsible for establishing patriarchal society. The severed head in the hand of a mother-goddess is a stark reminder that the bestower of life is also the bestower of mortality.

Those who live in villages prefer worshipping the domesticated form of the village goddess—the Gramadevi—who is perceived as the local manifestation of the cosmic mother-goddess. Every village in India has its very own Gramadevi. The village is usually named after her. The goddess of Mumbai is Mumbadevi; the goddess of Calcutta is Kali; the goddess of Chandigarh is Chandi. The goddess is represented by her head and two arms raised to bless the village. The villagers live on domesticated earth, which is the body of the goddess. Their homes, fields, and pastures are thus tamed aspects of the earth-goddess.

Women who die at childbirth, who are rejected by their husbands or society, or who die without experiencing conjugal or maternal bliss are identified with the Gramadevi. Kannagi, Renuka, Bahuchera, Manasi, Mari, and Dayamava are all manifestations of Gramadevi, the primal goddess who was forced into domestication by male gods:

Ammavaru created Shiva, Vishnu, and Brahma of her own body and desired to have sex with them. Vishnu and Brahma refused. Shiva agreed if she gave him her third eye. In her passion, Ammavaru gave away her third eye, the source of her primordial power. She became weak, and Shiva conquered her. From her body emerged all the village goddesses.

Folklore from southern India

Every year, during the annual village festival that is usually celebrated after harvest, the god-

dess goes through a period of ritual "widowhood." This period is marked not with mourning, but with sexual and violent ceremonies. Men from the lower castes use crude language to describe the genitals of the goddess and her insatiable sexual appetite. Male animals—goats, cocks, buffaloes—are slaughtered, their blood mixed with rice and sprinkled on the fields. Men of the village walk on fire and indulge in rituals of self-mutilation such as hook swinging. Women go through hysterical fits, shaking convulsively. Those around declare that the goddess has entered the body of these women. Promises are made to please the goddess, and her advice is sought on various problems.

The "widowhood" releases the goddess from male control. She shrugs off her domesticated mantle and returns to her primal, wild, forest state in which her sexual desire is unbridled. The hysterical fits of the village woman are physical manifestations of mental repression. Crude comments on the sexuality of the goddess arouse her. Blood sacrifices are made to satisfy her roused libido. The rituals of sex and violence restore the fertility of the goddess, which can then be utilized by the village in the year after the goddess has been redomesticated through the ritual of remarriage.

The following story of the southern Indian goddess Virapanchali, the divine aspect of the Pandava queen Draupadi, captures the idea that consumption of blood satisfies the sexual urge of the goddess and that maternity domesticates her:

During their exile in the forest, the Pandava Bhima complained to Krishna that he could not satisfy his wife sexually and felt inadequate as a result. Krishna revealed to Bhima that the Pandavas' wife was the primal mother-

goddess Adya-Maya-Shakti. One night the Pandavas discovered that Draupadi was not in her bed. They searched the forest and discovered her running wild and naked in the forest, eating goats, buffaloes, and other wild animals. When she saw her husbands spying on her, she ran toward them, intending to catch and eat them, too. The Pandavas ran for cover and sought refuge in their hut. They shut the door and refused to let Draupadi in until she promised not to harm them. She agreed and Bhima opened the door. Draupadi gripped his hand so hard that her five fingernails pierced his skin and five drops of blood fell on the ground. These turned into children and, hearing them cry, Draupadi's fury abated; she became maternal and loving again.

Telegu and Tamil folk versions
of the epic Mahabharata

Blood, like semen, is considered creative essence. In Ayurveda, semen is viewed as transformed blood. Thus, offerings of male blood are, in effect, offerings of semen.

Ceremonies aimed at pleasing the goddess through blood sacrifices are also conducted whenever the village is struck with disease or drought, which is seen as the manifestations of divine wrath and female frustration.

The ritual torture of male members of the village is a symbolic apology for cruelties meted out in the name of social order. After all, it is in the name of social order that women are forced into unhappy marriages or rejected on grounds of adultery and disobedience.

Two-Faced Mother

One of the most stunning representations of the goddess is that of Chinnasmastika. There are no sacred narratives associated with this goddess, who is often depicted standing headless upon a couple making love. She holds a sword in one hand and her head in other. Three streams of blood spurt out of her neck, two into the mouths of attending yoginis and one into her own mouth. The image shows sex and violence, life and death as aspects of the interdependent system that is Nature. The image jolts the viewer into accepting that the mother-goddess is also the killer-goddess. The two make up the whole.

Chinnamastika is not worshipped by orthodox Hindus who follow the Vedantic tradition, where the world is seen as maya, or delusion, and the aspirant seeks a transcendent truth. They prefer to view the goddess as a demure and domesticated consort. In the Tantrik tradition, however, the world is seen as shakti, or the source of power, and the goddess is invoked in her totality. The aspirant is asked not to bridle his senses. Instead he is sensually aroused and intimidated by both alluring and repulsive manifestations of the goddess. He is forced to confront and come to terms with the beauty and ugliness of the world within and the world without. Ultimately, it is hoped, he realizes that beauty and ugliness, sacrality and profanity, creation and destruction, are merely points of view. The realization enlightens and empowers.

Another image of the goddess that captures her entirety is that of Bhagavati, a manifestation of the goddess worshipped mainly in the southern state of Kerala. The goddess is depicted as a full-breasted, broad-hipped damsel with shapely eyes who bears many weapons in her many arms and has fangs for teeth. This image of the goddess attracts and repels. Suddenly one realizes that Nature is not just the voluptuous body; it is also the putrefying flesh. Nature is both the parrot and the maggot, the

Naked with hair unbound, Chinnamastika severs her head and drinks her own blood as she makes love to her consort, Bhairava—thus uniting the principles of impersonal violence and sex that rotate the cycle of life. Kangra painting. Eighteenth century.

cow and the scorpion. One enjoys spring blossoms but refuses to believe that the fragrance, color, and nectar are nothing but sex tools that ensure pollination by birds and bees. One prefers to see Nature as the nymph who enchants and as the mother who loves. One adores her broad hips and suckles her full breasts but shrinks from claws, fanglike teeth, and her lolling, blood-soaked tongue. One can see the weapons in her hand but prefers to believe she decapitates only demons and bad people.

But there are no "bad" people in the Hindu universe. There is no Satan in Hindu lore. The demons, like the gods, are the sons of Prajapati. The "gods" are known as adityas after their mother Aditi, while the "demons" are known

as daityas after their mother Diti. Aditi means "fetterless one," suggesting that the adityas are unfettered, free, unbound to the laws of space and time. The daityas, then, are the "fettered ones," trapped in space and time, and hence in constant battle with their favored half-brothers. The word *deva* applied to the adityas is translated as "god," which is more often than not just a convenient translation; it actually means "keeper of light." Another word for "demons" is *asuras*—"those who were denied the elixir of immortality." The asuras are merely anti-devas, opposing everything the "gods" do. The gods ensure the flow of rasa. The demons block it. The demons represent darkness, disorder, desire, bondage, and barrenness. They display behavior attributed to "evil" beings in Judaism, Christianity, and Islam. But Hinduism does not acknowledge "evil" in the Judeo-Christian-Islamic sense of the term. Negative events are attributed to negative karma. There is no need for the Devil. There is no clear demarcation between right and wrong in Hindu lore, just as there is no well-defined beginning or end. The Hindu universe remains a mystery and cannot be forced into a duality.

In sacred lore the demons who are killed by the mother-goddess are often ambitious, deva-hating celestial beings who seek to subvert natural law and avert death, becoming as immortal as the devas. They win boons from their father, Brahma, for this purpose:

The demon Daruka could be killed neither by man nor by gods, neither by birds nor by beasts, neither by plants nor by rocks. He did not seek protection from women, because he did not consider women a threat. Realizing this, the gods called upon the mother-goddess. Riding onto the battlefield on a lion, bearing in her many arms a trident, a lance, a sword, a bow, and many arrows, the goddess challenged Daruka to a fight. She frightened him with her red eyes and dark skin. He saw her ride a mad elephant, holding aloft the impaled bodies of her victims. Terrified, Daruka ran. The goddess stopped him. Taking the form of Bhagavati, she thrust her trident into his heart. She cut off his head, drank his blood, decorated herself with his entrails, and danced on his corpse. The gods cheered her victory.

Folklore from the
state of Kerala

Nature triumphs ultimately. The triumph is impersonal, nonjudgmental. Nature kills everybody, not just the "bad." To call the goddess "Mother" is to acknowledge only one half of her personality. She is also a "killer." She is the source of joy and sorrow, of hope and despair, life and death. Nature (prakriti), delusion (maya), energy (shakti)—she is the world we react to.

A Brief History of Hinduism

?–3000 B.C.E.

Primitive substratum of cave dwellers and forest tribes who worship ancestors, plants, animals, mountains, lakes, rivers, stones, and forest spirits known as yakshas

3000–2000 B.C.E.

Rise and fall of goddess-worshipping city-states in the Indus River valley that had trade links with Mesopotamia

2000–1200 B.C.E.

Rise in northern India of militaristic and pastoral Vedic culture, which invokes celestial spirits known as devas through the ritual of yagna to satisfy material aspirations

1200–600 B.C.E.

Gradual spread of Vedic culture to eastern and southern India; increasing domination of Vedic society by the priestly class; caste hierarchies formulated; Brahmanical orthodoxy established in Hindu society

800–500 B.C.E.

Ascetic revolution of the Upanishads followed by rise of monastic orders, such as Buddhism and

Jainism; intellectual speculation rife as scholars and seers debate on the true nature of cosmos and divinity; ritualism loses ground

800 B.C.E.–200 C.E.

Increasing popularity of hero cults, such as those of Krishna and Rama; composition of epics and legends that have greater mass appeal than erudite philosophical speculation; folk gods, popular rituals, and tribal beliefs gradually make inroads into the classical traditions

500 B.C.E.–400 C.E.

Crystallization of six major schools of Hindu philosophy—Yoga, Samkhya, Vedanta, Mimansa, Nyaya, Vaiseshika; contact with Persia and the Magi sun worshippers; trade links established with Rome over land and sea; sophisticated Sangam culture evolves in the south that patronizes Brahmanism, Buddhism, and Jainism

300 B.C.E.–200 C.E.

Hordes of Indo-Greeks, Scythians, and Parthians from central Asia follow Alexander into northern India and gradually get absorbed in the local culture; introduction of idol worship; spread of Buddhism across India and to China via central Asia; Saint Thomas brings Christianity to India, first to the Indus valley, then to the west coast of Kerala

200–800 C.E.

Classical age of Hindu culture; gradual collapse of Buddhism; rise of theistic schools; establishment of Shaiva and Vaishnava traditions; spread of Hinduism to southeastern Asia; popularization of temple culture

400–600 C.E.

Invasion and absorption of Huns and Gujar tribes from northwest; rise of Rajput militaristic traditions in western and central India; rise of social and religious feudalism

500–900 C.E.

Stranglehold of Brahmanical patriarchal values based on Manu Smriti and Dharmashastras; caste identity becomes inflexible; concepts of ritual purity and untouchability gain ground; stories of gods, kings, and sages compiled in Puranas; Tantrik practices exert influence on popular rituals such as vratas and pujas; Arab trading vessels ply western coast; cultural isolation of India

800–1500 C.E.

Doctrine of devotion spreads from southern to northern India; sophisticated philosophical commentaries on Vedanta written by Shankara—later elaborated on by Ramanuja, Madhava, Vallabha—forms its intellectual bedrock; massive temple complexes built in the east and the south as devotional cults acquire royal patronage; vernacular religious literature fires the imagination of the people

1000–1700 C.E.

Central Asian Muslim warlords invade India; persecution of Hindus in the north; establishment of Muslim kingdoms; Islam becomes major political and intellectual force in India; belief in heaven, hell, submission, and redemption becomes popular in Hinduism

1500–1800 C.E.

Arrival of Europeans by sea; rise in the economic and political power of Portugal, France, and finally England; introduction of Christian missions and Western education

1700–1900 C.E.

Hindu renaissance in the educated middle class; reappraisal of orthodox customs, beliefs, and rituals; preference for Hindu philosophy

1800–2000 C.E.

Appreciation of Hindu culture in the West; rise in Hindu nationalism and fundamentalism

Dates of Hindu Scriptures

SCRIPTURES	CONTENT	APPROXIMATE PERIOD OF FINAL COMPILATION
Rig Veda	Hymns to divine spirits	1500–1200 B.C.E.
Atharva Veda	Occult chants	1000–900 B.C.E.
Brahmanas	Ritual manuals	900–700 B.C.E.
Jatakas	Tales of Buddha's past lives	400–300 B.C.E.
Sutras	Philosophical aphorisms	400 B.C.E.–500 C.E.
Mahabharata	Epic related to Krishna	300 B.C.E.–300 C.E.
Ramayana	Epic related to Rama	200 B.C.E.–200 C.E.
Panchatantra	Tales of worldly wisdom	200–600 C.E.
Kamasutra	Erotic manual	400–500 C.E.
Dharmashastra	Law books	400–800 C.E.
Puranas	Theistic lore	500–1500 C.E.
Tantras	Manuals on the occult	500–1200 C.E.
Agamas	Treatises on Theism (Shaiva, Vaishnava, and Shakta traditions)	500–1200 C.E.
Katha-sarit-sagar	Tales of worldly wisdom	1000 C.E.

Glossary

Adi-Ananta-Sesha	Serpent of time
Aditi	Mother of the devas
Adya	Primal mother-goddess
Agni	God of fire
akshaya	Inexhaustible
Akupara	Turtle who forms the foundation of the universe
amrita	Nectar of immortality; ambrosia
apsaras	Divine damsels; celestial courtesans
artha	Material weath; principle of economics and politics
asana	Postures that redirect the energies of the body for mystical and occult purposes
asuras	Netherworld spirits; eternal enemies of the devas
banyan	Fig tree (*Ficus religiosa*)

bhakti	Devotion, a type of yoga
Brahma	God of creation
brahmacharya	Continence
Brahman	Impersonal unmanifest directive principle of the cosmos; spirit; pure consciousness; ultimate divine
brahmana	Priest; highest caste in the Hindu caste heirarchy
Brahmanas	Ritual manuals
Buddha	Title of Sakyamuni Siddhartha Gautama, the founder of Buddhism
buddha	Enlightened one
Buddhism	Path of the enlightened; non-Hindu monastic order that originated in India
devas	Keepers of light and order; guardians of fertility; usually described as gods
dharma	Worldly obligations; laws that maintain order and stability in society and the cosmos
gandharvas	Celestial musicians; masculine aspects of Nature's sensuality and fertility
garbha	Womb
garbhadhana	Conception
grihastha	Householder
Indra	Leader of the devas
Itihasas	Epics containing legendary history: Ramayana, Mahabharata, and Harivamsa
Jainism	Path of the true conquerors; non-Hindu monastic religion that evolved in India

Jambudvipa	Ancient name for India that means "rose-apple continent"
Jatakas	Stories of the Buddha in his previous life
kalasha	Pot
Kama	God of love and lust
kama	Pleasure; sex
kanya	Prepubescent girl
karma	Actions that generate reactions and fetter the soul to the cycle of life
katha	Story; folktale
Krishna	Incarnation of Vishnu; a cowherd-god who herds all beings to the path of dharma
kshatriya	Warrior; nobleman
Kubera	Leader of the yakshas; guardian of gold and gems
kumbha	Jar
kumari	Single woman; virgin
Laxmi	Goddess of wealth, fortune, beauty, prosperity
linga	Aniconic phallic stone
lingam	Penis
lokapala	Guardians of the directions
lokas	Celestial realms
Mahabharata	A long epic culminating in a great battle won by the righteous Pandavas over the Kauravas
Mandara	Central mountain of the Hindu world, sometimes identified as Mount Kailas; abode of Shiva; axis of space

maya	Mirage; illusory nature of the world; delusion
Meru	Another name for Mandara
moksha	Release from the cycle of rebirths
nagas	Subterranean serpent beings
Parvati	Princess of the mountains; consort of Shiva
patra	Vessel
pipal	Fig tree (*Ficus indica*)
pitris	Ancestors; forefathers
prakriti	Nature; material reality; feminine being
pranayama	Breath control
Puranas	Chronicles of gods, kings, and sages
purna	Overflowing
purusha	Masculine being; spiritual reality
rakshasas	Wild forest spirits; barbarians
Ramayana	Epic of Rama, supreme upholder of dharma
rasa	Sap of life
Rati	Goddess of erotica
rishi	Sage; seer; hermit; one who performs tapasya; often married, though prefers celibacy
ritu	Nature's cycle
rudraksha	Sacred beads of the Shaiva
samadhi	Release from material reality

samsara	Cycle of life; material world
samskara	Rite of passage
Sandhya	Goddess of twilight
sanyasa	renunciation
sanyasi	Ascetic; hermit; monk
Sarasvati	Goddess of knowledge and the arts
Sati	Shiva's first wife who, unable to withstand her husband's humiliation by her father, killed herself
sati	Chaste wife
Shakti	Goddess of energy
shakti	Power
Shaiva	Related to Shiva
Shiva	God of destruction and transcendence
shudra	Serf; laborer; lowest caste in the Hindu social hierarchy
siddhi	Power to manipulate the forces of Nature
simanta	Hair-parting ceremony in the seventh month of pregnancy
tala	Nether region
Tantra	Occult sciences of Hinduism
tapas	Heat born of continence
tapasya	Austerities that generate tapas
Tirthankara	Jain pathfinder who leads one out of samsara
tulsi	Sacred basil plant

Upanishads	Philosophical treatises
Ushas	Goddess of dawn
Vaishnava	Related to Vishnu
vaishya	Merchant; moneyed person; third highest caste of the Hindu caste heirarchy
vanaprastha	Retirement
Varuna	God of the sea
Vayu	God of the wind
Vedanta	Philosophical school of Hinduism that represents the acme of the Vedas
Vedas	Holiest books of Hinduism, containing mystical and occult hymns
Vishnu	God who sustains the universe
vrata	Ritual vow involving fasting and all-night vigil taken for material and spiritual benefit
yagna	Ancient Vedic rite seeking to invoke and appease the gods
yakshas	Mysterious forest spirits who guard treasures
yoga	Practice of mind-body control for mystical and occult ends
yogini	Virgin attendants of the goddess
yoni	Female generative organ; womb; vulva

Select Bibliography

Abbot, J. E., and N. R. Godbole. *Stories of Indian Saints*. Delhi: Motilal Banarsidass Publishers Pvt. Ltd., 1996.

Anderson, Leona M. *Vasantotsava: The Spring Festivals of India*. New Delhi: D. K. Printworld (P) Ltd.,1993.

Dange, Sadashiv Ambadas. *Encyclopaedia of Puranic Beliefs and Practices*, vols. 1–5. New Delhi: Navrang, 1990.

Eliade, Mircea. *Myths, Dreams & Mysteries*. London: Collins, 1974.

Granoff, Phyllis, ed. *The Clever Adulteress and Other Stories*. Oakville, Ontario: Mosaic Press, 1990.

Gupta, Shakti M. *Plant Myths and Tradition in India*. New Delhi: Munshiram Manoharlal Publishers Pvt. Ltd., 1991.

Hawley, J. S., and D. M. Wulff, eds. *The Divine Consort*. Boston: Beacon Press, 1982.

Highwater, Jamake. *Myth & Sexuality*. New York: Meridian, 1990.

Hiltebeitel, Alf. *Cult of Draupadi,* vol. 1. Chicago: The University of Chicago Press, 1988.

Hiltebeitel, Alf, ed. *Criminal Gods and Demon Devotees*. New York: State University of New York Press, 1989.

Hopkins, E. Washburn. *Epic Mythology*. Delhi: Motilal Banarsidass Publishers Pvt. Ltd., 1986.

Jakimowicz-Shah, Marta. *Metamorphosis of Indian Gods*. Calcutta: Seagull Books, 1988.

Jayakar, Pupul. *The Earth Mother*. New Delhi: Penguin Books, 1989.

Kinsley, David. *Hindu Goddesses*. Delhi: Motilal Banarsidass Publishers Pvt. Ltd., 1987.

Kosambi, Damodar Dharmanand. *Myth and Reality*. Mumbai, India: Popular Prakashan Pvt. Ltd., 1994.

Mani, Vettam. *Puranic Encyclopaedia*. Delhi: Motilal Banarsidass Publishers Pvt. Ltd., 1996.

Mazumdar, Subash.*Who Is Who in the Mahabharata*. Mumbai, India: Bharatiya Vidya Bhavan, 1988.

Meyer, Johann Jakob. *Sexual Life in Ancient India*. Delhi: Motilal Banarsidass Publishers Pvt. Ltd., 1989.

O'Flaherty, Wendy Doniger. *Siva: The Erotic Ascetic*. London: Oxford University Press Paperbacks, 1981.

O'Flaherty, Wendy Doniger, tr. *Hindu Myths*. New Delhi: Penguin Books, 1975.

Pandey, Rajbali. *Hindu Samskaras*. Delhi: Motilal Banarsidass Publishers Pvt. Ltd., 1969.

Pattanaik, Devdutt. *Shiva—An Introduction*. Mumbai, India: Vakil, Feffer & Simons Pvt. Ltd., 1997.

————. *Vishnu—An Introduction*. Mumbai, India: Vakil, Feffer & Simons Pvt. Ltd., 1999.

Sen, Makhan Lal. *The Ramayana of Valmiki*. New Delhi: Munshiram Manoharlal Publishers Pvt. Ltd., 1978.

Subramaniam, Kamala. *Srimad Bhagavatam*. Mumbai, India: Bharatiya Vidya Bhavan, 1987.

Thadani, Giti. *Sakhiyani*. London: Cassell, 1996.

Walker, Benjamin. *Hindu World*, vols.1–2. New Delhi: Munshiram Manoharlal Publishers Pvt. Ltd., 1983.

Wilkins, W. J. *Hindu Mythology*. Delhi: Rupa & Company, 1997.

Zimmer, Heinrich. *Myths and Symbols in Indian Art and Civilization*. Delhi: Motilal Banarsidass Publishers Pvt. Ltd., 1990.

Thank you to Ki. Rajanarayanan for letting me use the story from Tamil folklore on page 135